Predjama Castle
A MEDIEVAL

The Postojna Cave
THE BEAUTY OF THE UNDERGROUND

POSTOJNSKA JAMA

Jamska c. 30, SLO-6230 Postojna
tel.: + 386 5/700 01 00, fax: + 386 5/700 01 30
e-mail: info@postojnska-jama.si; http://www.postojna-cave.com

Tourist Information Centre
Ljubljana - TIC

- Information and publicity editions on Ljubljana (brochures, maps, calendar of events), souvenirs
- Sightseeing tours (regular, on request)
- Tours by boat, tourist train
Basic information and publicity editions on Slovenia

Open:
1 June - 30 September: 8.00 - 21.00
1 October - 31 May: 8.00 do 19.00

Tourist Information Office
Trg OF 6 (Railway Station)

tel. in fax 01/433 94 75
e-mail: tic.zp@tera.net

Open:
1 June - 30 September: 8.00 - 22.00
1 October - 31 May: 10.00 do 19.00

TURISTIČNI INFORMACIJSKI CENTER LJUBLJANA
Stritarjeva ulica, 1000 Ljubljana, Slovenija
tel. +386 (0)1 306 12 15, fax +386 (0) 1 306 12 04
e-mail: tic@ljubljana-tourism.si, www.ljubljana.si

LJUBLJANA

SLOVENIA

The Sixth edition
Kranj, 2003

Text and photos by: Matjaž Chvatal
Maps by: Geodetski zavod Slovenije
Text editing by: Saša Poljak
Translated by: Simona Pečnik Kržič

Turistika Publising House, 2003
For the publisher: Mira Chvatal

Založba Turistika
Trstenik 101
4204 Golnik, Slovenia
Telephone: 00386 (0)64 460 110
E-mail: info@zalozba-turistika.si
http://www.turistika.net

CIP - Kataložni zapis o publikaciji
Narodna in univerzitetna knjižnica, Ljubljana

913(497.4)(036)

CHVATAL, Matjaž
   Slovenija. (Vodnik) / (text and photos by Matjaž Chvatal ;
Maps by Geodetski zavod Slovenije). - Kranj : Turistika, 1998

ISBN 961-90088-5-5

75677696

CONTENTS

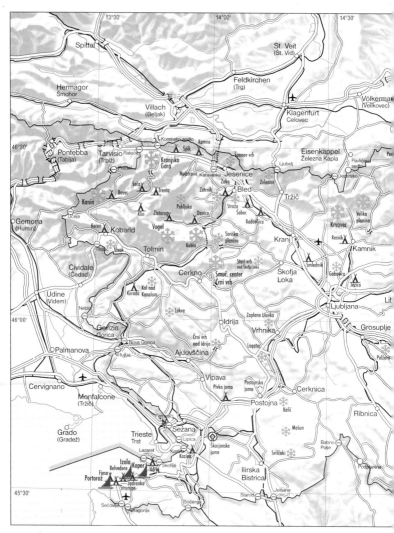

General Information about Slovenia

Slovenia is a small Central European country covering an area of only 20.256 km2 and with some two million inhabitants. It lies between the latitudes of 46°53' and 45°25' north and between the longitudes of 12°23' and 16°36' east at the crossroads of the Alps, the South-Eastern Europe and the Mediterranean. It borders Austria (330 km), Croatia (670 km), Italy (232 km) and Hungary (102 km). Total length of state borders is 1334 km, 413 km of them run on the rivers. Slovenia has 46.6 km of coastline. The highest peak is Triglav (2.864 m) and the highest mountain pass is the Vršič saddle (1611) (both in the Julian Alps). The largest lake is the intermittent Lake Cerknica (Cerkniško jezero) in Notranjska (Inner Carniola), lying at an altitude of 552 m, with a depth of up to 10.7 m and a surface of 2400 hectares. The deepest lake is Lake Bohinj (Bohinjsko jezero) in Gorenjska (Upper Carniola) with a depth of up to 44.5 m, a surface of 318 hectares and lying at an altitude of 526 m.

Slovenia, with its relatively small surface displays so many different types of landscape and climate as hardly any other country. The Alps stretching with their ridges into Slovenia from the north and north-west descend into wine-growing hills at the

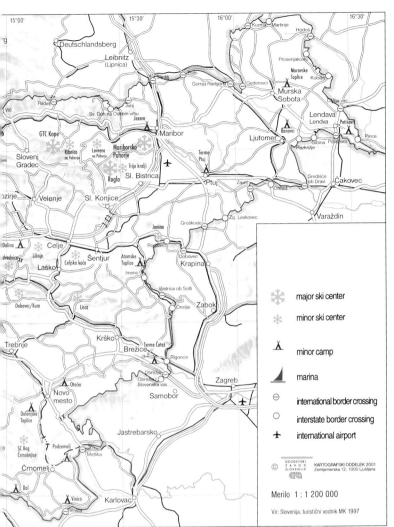

❄	major ski center
✳	minor ski center
⚑	minor camp
◢	marina
⊖	international border crossing
○	interstate border crossing
✈	international airport

edge of the Pannonian Plain in the east. Towards the south they lower into the wooded karstified Dinaric Mountains, which begin in Slovenia and parallelly to the Adriatic sea extend deep into the Balkan peninsula. And a small part of Slovene territory reaches all the way to the Adriatic sea.

Slovene climate is just as varied as is landscape. It covers all types of climate, from sub-Mediterranean, Alpine, Dinaric, to continental-Pannonian. Central Slovenia has a Central European climate. There's enough precipitation over all seasons. The territory in the east opens towards the Pannonian Plain and has continental climate with hot summers, cold winters and a smaller amount of precipitation. The higher we go in the Alps, the harsher the climate. Long snowy winter changes fast into a mild summer. This is an area abounding in precipitation. Mediterranean climate is typical of the territory between the Adriatic and the high karst plateaus. Those parts are sun-kissed in summer and kept warm by the sea in winter.

The landscape and the climate offer conditions for regional fauna. In the forests, covering half of the Slovene territory (which is far above European average), there is a lot of red and roe deer. In the Kočevsko and Notranjska forests lynx and brown bear can still be found. In steep precipices in the Alps we meet ibex, mouflons and numerous flocks of chamois, while hunting grounds on the edge of the Pannonian basin are rich in small game and birds. Practically everywhere you can find boars, hares, pheasants, foxes and various other kinds of small game. The fauna of the karst underground, where animals have adapted to living conditions by loosing their pigment and eyesight, is also very interesting. Proteus anguinus or "the human fish" is practically a symbol of Slovenia.

The longest river is the Sava with 221 km of its current running through the Slovene territory. The Drava runs through Slovenia for 144 km, the Kolpa for 118 km, the Savinja for 102 km, the Mura for 98 km, the Soča for 96 km, the Krka for 94 km, the Sotla for 90 km. There is also a number of shorter clear alpine rivers, streams and disappearing karst rivers rich in flora, and slow Pannonian rivers that run through Slovene valleys. Together with over 150 lakes and fishponds they offer numerous kinds of interesting fish for sports fishing.

The Triglav National Park is a large protected area in the central region of the Julian Alps covering 83807 hectares. Beside this protected natural park there are ten protected regional parks in Slovenia. They cover smaller interesting areas: in the Gorica region the Čaven-Trnovski gozd Park (4776 hectares) and Zgornja Idrijca Park

(4195 hectares), between the Gorica region and Notranjska the Nanos Park (2632 hectares), and at the coast the Sečovlje salt pans Park (835 hectares). In the Savinja region we find three regional parks: the Golte (1148 hectares), the Logar valley, 2475 hectares) and the valley Robanov kot (1423 hectares). In Koroška (Carinthia) there is the regional park

Basic Data on Slovenia

STATE:
Official name:
Republic of Slovenia
Capital city:
Ljubljana
Area:
20.256 km2
Geography:
The Alps in the northwest, the Panonnian Plain in the east, The Dinaric Mountains in the south, The Adriatic in the south-west.
Climate:
Sub-Mediterranean, Alpine, Pannonian, Dinaric

Topla (1368 hectares) and the smallest regional park is in Bela Krajina (White March) - the Lahinja Park (260 hectares).

We shouldn't forget to mention the renowned forest Krakovski gozd between Dolenjska (Lower Carniola) and Posavje (the Sava basin), the largest flatland forest in Slovenia, part of which is a genuine primeval forest.

Another primeval forest can be found in the Kočevski Rog. And last but not least, we should also mention the green Pohorje Massif, the Notranjska forests and Snežnik, all of them a veritable treasure of loveliness which seems to be long forgotten in industrialized countries.

The highest mountain:
Triglav, 2864 m
The lowest point:
sea level

ORDER:
Political order:
Democratic Republic
Head of the State:
President of the Republic
Head of the Government:
Prime Minister
Administrative division:
62 administrative districts

Legislation:
parliament with 90 members
state council with 40 members
Judicial system:
constitutional court, supreme court, circuit courts

POPULATION:
Population:
1 991 169 (30 June 1996)
Language:
Slovene
Currency:
Slovene tolar

Tourism

For such a small country, Slovenia boasts an extremely varied landscape. There is just a short pop from snow-capped mountains and glacial lakes in the Alps to evergreen olive plantations at the coast. And a drive to wine growing hills, golden wheat-fields or mysterious karst caves will not take us more than an hour, either. The country with its picturesqueness and diversity is just tempting us to stop and indulge in its treasures.

This is why the Slovenes have turned into a real "trip-making" nation. Wherever they choose to go, they can go on a trip. Mountaineering has been a tradition here for over 200 years. Slovene Mountains are dotted with almost 200 mountain huts and mountaineering societies count over 100.000 members.

Numerous farmhouses on the fringes of the Alps, in the Pohorje Massif, in the Savinja valley and elsewhere in Slovenia have wide opened their doors to visitors. A holiday in traditional farming environment of such farms which offer traditional home made food is the real thing. Guests used to industrialized environment can relax and enjoy peace and quiet to their hearts' content.

Inns have always been an essential part of the Slovene tradition. They were the place where people gathered, talked and had fun. Big things happened there and every tourist should stop at least once at the local inn, taste a genuine local dish and have some excellent Slovene wine.

In vino veritas - this saying is well at home in Slovenia. Vine grows in the east, south and west of the country. Wine-growing hills are criss-crossed with wine roads bringing a visitor to wine cellars and local culinary offer. Slovene wine, already well known by the ancient Romans, is today world-famous.

Famous wine growing regions are Podravje (the Drava region) comprising the south slopes of the Pohorje Massif,

It is only an easy hour and a half drive from Ljubljana to Portorož which makes the coast very attractive for numerous tourists. They spend a day, a week or a whole holiday at the seaside (top).

Fences protect gardens from numerous wild animals (top right).

Through Alpine valleys still flow rivers and streams so clean that you can drink from them. The Bistrica stream springs out under the 1000 meters high Triglav North Face (middle right).

The Slovene Kras is the cradle of world karstology. Karst caves have been attracting visitors for nearly 200 years. There is quite a number of caves that can be visited by tourists and in the Postojna cave there is even a small electric train. But an inexperienced visitor, accompanied by experienced potholers, can lately also explore unspoiled karst underground and descena into deep mysterious karst pits (bottom right).

the Slovenske Gorice between Ormož and Ljutomer, Maribor and the Haloze Hills.

The Bizeljsko-Sremiš wine region in Posavje (the Sava basin) is also famous for its wines. Žametna Črnina (a kind of dark grape) is typical of Bela Krajina, and Dolenjska is the homeland of Cviček (souerish wine). The best Cviček comes from Trška gora near Novo mesto.

Vineyards lend special charm to the littoral landscape in the Vipava valley, and the gently rounded hills of the Goriška brda are virtually unimaginable without vineyards.

Kraški Teran from Dutovlje and Tomaj and wines from the Koper district are also very much appreciated.

The spa tourism has quite a long tradition in Slovenia as well. It is not hard to guess when they first started to visit Rimske Toplice (the Roman Spa). Rogaška Slatina (Rogatec Mineral Spa) has been known for over 300 years and frequently visited by famous people, dignitaries as well as rulers, from all over Europe. The thermal spa Dobrna has just as long a tradition.

In Pomurje (the Mura region) we find the best-known Slovene spa Radenci and nearby are also the spas Moravske Toplice, Banovci and Terme Lendava.

Water springing in the spas Dolenjske Toplice and Šmarješke Toplice is so hot you can bathe there in an open swimming pool in the middle of the coldest winter. And the thermal spa Čateške Toplice offers its visitors a true bathing riviera.

Through ages, limestone, which is apt to dissolve in water, and dolomites gave birth to such magnificent karst phenomena, that the name of this type of Slovene landscape has become a technical term, and modern karstology developed on the basis of research done on Slovene territory.

There are nearly 7000 registered underground caves and pits in Slovenia. The longest is the Postojna cave system (Postojnska jama, 19.555 m), while the deepest pits can be found on Kanin and Rombon above Bovec. Their depths over 1000 meters rank them among the deepest in the world. The deepest pit in Slovenia has a depth of over 1.370 meters.

20 underground caves can be visited by tourists. Visitors have been taken into the Postojna cave since as early as 1818. Just as frequently visited as the Postojna cave are the Škocjan caves near Divača which are also inscribed in the UNESCO World Natural Heritage List. A visitor will never forget a boat ride through underground lakes of the magically beautiful Križna cave (Križna jama) near Lož. The snow white aragonite crystals resembling hedgehogs in the Raven cave (Ravenska jama) above Cerkno deserve to be mentioned as well. And the Snowy cave (Snežna jama) on Raduha is something really special.

Slovenia is a land of castles and some of them have even been turned into hotels (Podvin, Mokrice, Otočec). Castles are truly abundant. Some of them have been preserved and restored, some damaged in the course of time, yet others burnt down during the WW II. Bled Castle perched on the precipitous rock above the idyllic lake has already become a kind of a Slovenian symbol. Predjama Castle near Postojna is also very impressive. Škofja Loka and Ptuj Castles make part of the medieval town cores of Škofja Loka and Ptuj, respectively. The old pirate town of Piran offers its visitor an interesting stroll through its narrow streets in Mediterranean style. Numerous churches have grown on the hills over the last centuries, and today there are so numerous it is difficult to count them. Remains from earlier cultures like the Vače situla (a bucket-like vessel), Celtic arms, Illyrian jewelry and an abundance of Roman finds, can be found practically all over Slovenia.

A visitor will also find it hard to overlook traditional Slovene cooking. Dishes and eating habits are very varied in Slovenia. There are up to 40 different culinary regions with their typical dishes. The menu in Slovene kitchen boasts castle dishes as well as those typical of towns and simple farm food. Specialties are also dishes that used to be prepared by the Idrija miners, the Savinja Valley

The Piran peninsula stretches far into the sea between the Piran and Strunjan Bays. The old town core of Piran sits right at the very narrow end of the peninsula (top). Big Baroque Church of St. George is perched above the town (it was rebuilt in Baroque style in 1637). From the church, houses descend in rows all the way to the coast. Piran streets are narrow, really Mediterranean-like, paved with stones. Tartinijev trg, the center of Piran, was only built at the end of the 19th century after the inner port had been filled. Piran is a very popular tourist spot, a shelter for people who like to spend their time in noble and rich ancient ambience.

raftsmen, herdsmen, millmen, ... We should not forget, though, that in Slovenia pig is the king of animals. Almost throughout Slovenia, especially in the countryside, pork is the main food, while the koline (traditional annual killing of a pig) is a very festive occasion for the whole family. Therefore, traveler, do stop, open your eyes and you will see a small but friendly land and meet interesting people. You will be surprised at the wealth this country shyly hides in its bosom.

History

Centuries ago, Slovenia was inhabited by Illyrian tribes. Around 400 BC they were joined by the Celtic tribes. In 200 BC they were ruled over by the Romans, who built military fortifications along new roads all the way to the Danube. The Germanic Langhobards only settled in the territory when the power of the Roman Empire began to decline. After the downfall of the Roman Empire, at the end of the 6th century, the Langhobards moved east to Italy, and the provinces they abandoned were settled by our ancestors - the Slovenes. At the same time, Roman social order based on slavery came to its end. The Slovenes based their social order on old tribal structures.

Over a few following centuries the Slovenes lived in freedom. Their princes were elected in Gosposvetsko polje (Saalfeld in Austrian Carinthia). Slovene settlements were scarce and moreover, they were divided among different tribes which led to a complete overrule of their Germanic neighbours in the 10th century. The land was fragmented and given to foreign dignitaries, aristocratic families and the bishops of Brixen, Freising and Salzburg. In that period the Slovenes accepted Christian faith and culture.

It was not until the 16th century that national consciousness started to spring up among rare intelligentsia. The Slovene language was at first used only in Christian preaching. The first Slovene grammar book was published. In the 18th century, Slovene language came to a greater use.

During the "spring of nations" in 1848, the Slovene issue also came up in politics. A major character in the first political program called "Slovenia United" was the poet France Prešeren. After the downfall of the Habsburg Empire one third of the Slovene territory remained under Italy and the rest of it was together with Serbia and

Top: Slovene territory boasts a number of silent witnesses of its rich history which wasn't always pretty. One of them is the Kobarid Ossuary (top) of Italian soldiers who lost their lives during the WW I near Kobarid, and another one is the Kobarid Museum dedicated to the horrors of the Isonzo Front which claimed over 1.000.000 lives.

The streets of Ljubljana are full of joy and good mood. Slovenes are cheerful and friendly people (middle).

Ancient walls testify to the power of former towns (bottom).

Croatia united into a new country. Its social order was unitarian and centralist. Because of great cultural and national differences it could only be ruled by a strong hand. That state did not acknowledge all national rights to the Slovenes, either.

The second world war left deep scars in the Slovene nation. The Germans deported all intelligentsia, ecclesiastics and ten thousands of farmers. Their homes were given to German immigrants. The Slovene language was banned in public and from schools and churches, Slovene books were burnt and patriots shot.

Soon after the occupation first partisan units sprang up from the underground and became part of the Yugoslav partisan army led by the Communist Party under the leadership of Josip Broz Tito. This army was also recognized by the Russians, Americans and the British as their ally in the fight against the Germans.

After the WW II Slovenia as a part of Yugoslavia remained behind the iron curtain. Complete control was taken by the Communist Party. All companies and large estates were nationalized. Strict political control over society and centralized economy were introduced.

After 1948 borders slowly began to open and the strict control tended to become less strict. It was only after Tito's death in 1980 that modern civil society began to emerge in Slovenia. In those years Slovenia strongly resisted the resurrection of the strong hand of Belgrade.

On 23 December 1990, more than 88% of the voters voted for a sovereign independent state. After that Slovenia was no longer part of Yugoslavia. Six months after the promulgation of plebiscite results Slovenia became legally independent by the Basic Constitutional Charter.

Traditional Slovene Crafts

Traditional crafts have always provided man with household utensils, personal equipment and things he needed at work. All these products were also an important market merchandise. As for the locals, their work offered them possibilities to pave routes to distant lands and broaden their horizons.

Today traditional crafts hold a significant place in Slovenia, both economically and in national culture. Traditional craft is an important ingredient of Slovene cultural heritage. It reflects the influence different Slovene regions exerted on each other for centuries.

Slovene shoemaking industry has a strong back-up in traditional shoe-making in Tržič, Turnišče and Žiri, hatters in Škofja Loka while straw hats originate from Domžale and Mengeš.

Traditional shoe-making heritage is preserved in the museums in Tržič and Turnišče, the latter boasting an old reconstructed shoe-maker house. It shows the life and work of a shoemaker from Turnišče during the period between the two world wars.

Today, pottery is developed in Komenda, in Dolenjska, near Krško, at Ptuj, Ljutomer, Pešarovci, etc. Potters also sell their products at numerous fairs in different Slovene towns. Even today, they offer different clay pots and objects that were already used by our ancestors.

Ribničans have been peddling their suha roba (wooden utensils) around Europe since ever. They obtained permission to trade freely in their products as early as 1492. That enabled them to peddle in Austria, Hungary, Italy, Germany, Greece and Spain. They went even as far as Africa and India.

Today a suhorobar (woodsmith) from Ribnica can be met at every fair in Slovenia. In Ribnica, they annually

A Ribn'čan displays suha roba, this time in Bohinj (top). His products range from wicker baskets, graters and wooden spoons to straw hats, small planks and numerous other objects of useful or ornamental value for your home and household.

Small bread from Dražgoše (Dražgoški kruhek) is something special. Diligent hands of farmers' wives make honey dough and then the pastry (middle right) out of it. In Škofja Loka, dough is pressed into a carved wooden mould and baked.

In Slovenia, lace first appeared in Idrija and then spread to the Žiri basin and to Železniki (lace on the bottom picture). Lacemaking used to provide an important additional income in the miners', forgers' and charcoal burners' families. When the last furnace was extinguished (in 1902) in Železniki, lacemaking became the only source of income for numerous families. In those parts they still make lace. To keep the tradition alive they founded the Lacemaking school in Idrija. Lace differs in patterns and knots from town to town.

organize the Ribnica Fair and rich heritage of the woodsmiths is on display at the Ribnica Museum.

There is also a well known song about the suha roba and Ribničans "Ribn'čan Urban". Suhorobar actually became a symbol of our opening into the world and earning our living by making what we can out of what is at hand.

Traditional craft of making honey products also used to be called "krajcarkšeft" (kreutzer business) since candle makers and lectars (they made honey products) only dealed with small money.

Even today you will still find some family workshops with long tradition. Making small ornamented honey pastry is particularly developed in Škofja Loka and its surroundings, where those products are called small bread. In Škofja Loka the dough is pressed into handmade wooden moulds while in Dražgoše they are hand-made.

Coloured ornamented honey pastry is made in Ljubljana, Kamnik, Slovenj Gradec, Ptuj, Metlika and Ljutomer.

One of the oldest family crafts is wickerwork and not so long ago it was mastered in every household. Baskets, wickers and straw baskets were made during the winter in every family. Wickermakers mostly use hazel and willow twigs, but objects made of straw and corn husks are also very interesting.

Even today wickerwork is one of the most common crafts and numerous artisans offer a great variety of products.

Lacery began to develop in the 17th century in Idrija where we can find the only Lace-making School in Slovenia. This activity used to bring a more than welcome additional income to miners' families. Today, famous Lace-making towns are Idrija, Železniki and Žiri, while skillfully made lace from tireless lace makers is a greatly appreciated and demanded merchandise.

Slovene cooking

Slovene cooking is just as varied as the landscape. Old national dishes have rich tradition. Some of them have been preserved through centuries. In Slovenia there have around 40 culinary districts, which apart from having very different eating habits also have very different dishes. Soil composition and weather conditions varying from district to district have helped to shape nutrition of the inhabitants.

On the menu of the traditional Slovene cooking one will find refined and exquisite dishes that used to be served in castles, a rich choice of dishes from Slovene town cooking, a culinary treasure of Slovene farm cooking and dishes typical of various groups such as the Idrija miners, the Savinja Valley raftsmen, lumberjacks, parsonage cooking, etc.

Today, it's the simple elementary farm dishes that are most common in Slovene kitchens. All imagination and inventiveness put in them were preserved together with them. Dishes that used to make part of the festive menu of the Slovene farmer are even today a true feast for the eyes.

King of the animals in Slovenia

In Slovenia the pig is a veritable king of the animals as pork still represents the main food for the majority of the Slovenes. This is the reason why *koline* (traditional pig slaughtering and preparation of pork products) represents the biggest winter time feasts for a Slovene farmer. With *koline* go rich feasts, home-made culinary delicacies and numerous games and customs.

Especially nice custom is exchanging the koline (pork products) with the neighbours in order to taste them. Black pudding - sausages filled with a mixture of blood, intestines, millet and buckwheat porridge - are also very common throughout Slovenia and most frequently they are the object of neighbourly gifts.

Bread is very important to the Slovenes since there is practically no meal without bread. They are a nation of bread eaters. The tradition of home-made bread goes far back as well, and the day of the week when the bread was baked in the farm stove was a feast for the whole family (top). O, the sweet smell of freshly baked bread! But bread wasn't baked every day. It was usually made once for the whole week or an even longer period. Even today there are quite some farms where bread is only baked once a week. Cottagers, crofters and poorer farmers made bread from a mixture of black flour and potatoes. Such bread stayed fresh for several days.

Best known specialty in Slovenia is ham - cured pork leg. In Primorska (the Littoral) they make *pršut* - air-dried pork leg. One of the specialties is also *želodec* - a filled pork stomach, differently prepared in practically every region. Some of them are cured while others are simply air-dried.

Pomurje (the Mura region)

The menu of this district offers a large choice of soups, flour-based dishes and dishes made with dough. Cabbage,

Richer farmers used to make white bread with prunes, raisins, walnuts, sunflower and pumpkin seeds (bottom). No bread from the bakery can be as delicious as the bread baked in the traditional farm stove. Any visitor who will stop at one of the numerous tourist farmhouses can convice himself of that. They still serve genuine local food and drink. In the wine-growing regions that is premium wine, and in other parts guests are greeted with strong home made brandy, which is supposed to "tie down their soul". Sadly, the old tradition of welcoming guests with bread and salt has been abandoned.

turnip, beans, pumpkins, etc. are also widely used. In meat dishes, pork is most frequent, but one will also find quite some poultry (chickens, geese, ducks, turkey-hens) and home-bred rabbits. Their renowned dishes are *bograč* - a stew made of pork, beef, game and wine, *gibanica* (layer cake with curd cheese, walnuts, poppy seeds and apples), various soups and other dishes.

Štajerska (Styria)

A soup in this region is almost a must. Besides the renowned sour soup the region boasts a wide range of other varieties made of chicken and beef. In wine-growing hills they even make wine soup. From these parts originates roasted *martinova gos* (Martin's goose - prepared for St. Martin's day when the new wine is baptized) and *konjiški lonec* (a dish from Slovenske Konjice made with beef tail), *flosarski golaž* (rafter's stew) and *flosarski zrezek* (rafter's steak). The Upper Savinja Valley (Zgornja Savinjska dolina) is known for *žlinkrofi* (square shaped pasta with a meat stuffing).

Cabbage deserves to be mentioned as well since it is used in numerous dishes such as *pečeno štajersko zelje* (baked cabbage filled with minced meat and porridge and topped with sour cream), *štruklji* (made of rolled-out dough and stuffed with cabbage and then boiled) and *potica* (roll cake stuffed with cabbage). *Štruklji* stuffed with tarragon filling are also very typical of the region.

Koroška (Carinthia)

High mountain farms in Koroška still serve apple must, home made bread, sausages and cured ham, cheese and a small bowl of sour milk with buckwheat or corn *žganci* (made of different hard-boiled flour). In Koroška *žganci* are made in a special way: first, they stir-fry the flour, then they gradually add salted boiling water and grease.

Koroška is also renowned for its boiled štruklji with buckwheat filling and for *koroški mavžlje* made of the meat from pig's head, fried bread, buckwheat porridge and different kinds of spices, all together wrapped in pork net and roasted.

Gorenjska (Upper Carniola)

Even today, local cuisine is based on meat and milk. The region has always been closely connected with cattle-breeding and Alpine dairy farming and even today it is known for excellent cheese. The *ementalec* cheese from Bohinj is very famous while the smelly *mohant* is slightly less famous. The region is also known for its *orehova potica* (walnut roll), *šara* - hot pot with ram's legs and vegetables, and *gorenjska prata* made of chopped meat from a pig's head and diced bread, mixed with spices and eggs and roasted wrapped in pork net.

No other region could compete with Gorenjska when it came to the number of porridge dishes. But that was in the past, although it is true that even today Gorenjska boasts a great variety of boiled *štruklji*.

Nutrition in Slovene regions is very varied, be it sea-food delicacies (top) or žlikrofi. The Idrija žlikrofi (bottom) are filed with potatos, while elsewhere they can also be filled with meat and other stuffings.

Dolenjska and Posavje

The most typical Dolenjska dish is štruklji. The Slovenes are known for making štruklji in more than 70 different ways and quite a number of them originate from Dolenjsko. The region is also known for žlikrofi prepared with different stuffings (intestines, meat, cheese, eggs, poultry, etc.) and sauces.

There is also an abundance of other dishes such as grilled lambkins and piglets, typical of Bela Krajina, a goose or a turkey with chestnut stuffing, mesne pletenice, prosenice - smoked sausages made of pork entrails, meat and millet, tovorna potica, a roll-cake filled with sauerkraut and smoked pork or ham, and buckwheat potica from Bizeljsko filled with cottage cheese, cream and walnuts.

A specialty is also roasted pork ribs with baked potatoes. We also shouldn't forget about pork feet, home-made sausages cooked in wine, and dormice. Be it in a well seasoned goulash or stew, roasted with mashed chestnuts and apples, or boiled with potatoes, these tiny animals represent a true delicacy.

Notranjska (Inner Carniola)

The specialty of the region is *krompirjevi žganci*, made from potatoes and wheat or barley flour, as well as hot pots cooked in clay pots in traditional farm stoves: *ričet* (also called *ješprenj*), beans with bacon and the renowned *bloška trojka* seasoned with cracklings.

The region is also known for baked *štruklji* with cream, cured pike and millman's pike. Typical of the region are also notranjski želodec (pork stomach), lung and liver sausages.

Some inns hare pretty long tradition.

Cooks in Slovene inns can offer a number of home-style delicacies and spoil every guest, no matter how demanding he might be (bottom).

Primorska, the Kras and the Gorica region

In this area, soup has mainly been replaced by various types of pasta, although they offers dry soup with *pršut* and rice and a variety of fish soups and vegetable *mineštra* (minestrone) along the coast.

A strong influence of Mediterranean cuisine is felt throughout the region but despite that very particular and specific dishes have developed in different areas.

One of such areas is Idrijsko-Cerkljansko (the Idrija and Cerkno regions) known for old Idrija miners' dishes: *budle* - cornballs with raisins, dried turnip peels boiled with potatoes and also delicious *jetrne klobase* (liver sausages). The regional specialties are *žlikrofi* stuffed with a potato filling, and *bakalca* - a sauce made from ram or rabbit meat served with *žlikrofi*.

Polenta is well-known in the whole region although practically every village prepares it according to its own recipe. It is served with cottage cheese, fish *brodet* (Istrian fish stew), goulash, escargots in sauce, etc.

The region is also known for its vegetable side dishes - mangold with potatoes, peas with *pršut*, fennel fried in olive oil, aubergines and asparagus, prepared in every possible way.

Truffles are a true delicacy. This most precious and expensive mushroom in the world grows in Koper hinterland. Truffles are served stewed with herbs and wine in *fritajla*, in risotto, with pasta and in fish dishes.

Everybody in Primorska knows *bakalar* - mashed codfish with olive oil and garlic. The region is, naturally, the home of a number other sea food delicacies. Different kinds of shell-fish, crayfish, squid and fish prepared either in *buzara*, *brodets*, various marinades, or roasted or grilled also deserve mentioning.

Gorenjska

Gorenjska is a land of high peaks, pointed rocky ridges, deep Alpine valleys and clear waters. The landscape simply lures everyone who wants to escape for a while the hustle and bustle so typical of tourist centers. Here, quiet excitements can be found in the midst of unspoiled wild nature.

Gorenjska is a school of healthy living. Views from the heights extend to unimaginable distances. In hidden gorges we are greeted by thunder of waterfalls, in valleys by still lakes. Merry mountaineering adventures await for us here as well as quiet enjoyment.

This outstandingly Alpine landscape offers numerous leisure time activities. Walking, mountain-climbing, horse-riding, golf, rafting, para gliding, winter joys, hunting, fishing as well as some other activities can liven up our days in every season.

Kranj

Steep river banks and conglomerate promontory above the confluence of the Sava and Kokra rivers used to offer excellent defence conditions in ancient times. On this remarkable strategic position a town was built, a town which gained importance already in the early Middle Ages. It was the seat of country counts of the Kranj County.

The Town Hall houses a museum and numerous buildings in the old town core are preserved. The old cemetery, where the greatest Slovene poet, dr. France Prešeren, is buried, has been turned into a park. The Kokra river has cut a narrow and picturesque gorge through the very center of Kranj.

Atop Šmarjetna gora above Stražišče sits a hotel. Another popular outing spot of the locals is Jošt (845 m).

Near Kranj, the Sava enters the mighty Zarice gorge. It is dammed at Mavčiče and the dam for Mavčiče hydro power station has a surface of 1 km^2.

The main street in the center of Kranj is a pedestrian zone. It carries the name of the lawyer and greatest Slovene poet, dr. France Prešeren (1800-1849), who spent his last years in one of the houses in the street. The first floor of the house now has a memorial room and the first floor and the cellar house a gallery (top right).

High up on the steep slope of the Jelovica plateau lie the villages of Jamnik and Kolombart. Between them, right at the end of a barren ridge sits the Church of St. Primus (831 m) with great views of the Gorenjska Plain and the hills behind it. In the background is Storžič (2132 m) (middle right).

At the edge of Kokrica, a Kranj suburb, was once a big clay pit. After they stopped digging clay, the pits were filled with water, thus making three fishponds. The larger two are Krokodilnica (bottom right) and Čukova jama, and the small one is shyly hiding in the bushes. The fishponds are protected as a nature bird reserve.

On the plain, in the direction of Kamnik, is situated the main Slovene international airport Aerodrom Ljubljana.

Further up from Kranj the Sava flows through a narrow valley with a railroad running parallel to the river. On the west bank we find the village of Besnica and on the right bank, in a small dry valley between Dobrava and the Udenboršt forest, lies Naklo.

The village of Predoslje is situated near Kranj in the direction of the Karavanke Chain. Near the village lies the well-known Brdo castle which has a large park with eleven lakes. Near Kokrica, a small village between Kranj and Predoslje, is the nature reserve - the Bobovek fishponds.

Under the slopes of Kriška gora and Storžič lies Golnik - a health resort with a sanatorium specialized in lung diseases. Preddvor with its castles whose task was to protect entrance into the Kokra Valley, and its artificial lake Črnjava are becoming an increasingly popular tourist spot. Terraced peaks separated by deep ravines boast small hilltop churches of St. Jacob (960), St. Nicholas (651) and St. Lawrence (829).

From Preddvor towards Cerklje you find several villages under the slopes of Štefanja gora (748): Velesovo with its monastery, Češnjevek with its fishponds and Cerklje with the nearby Strmol Castle. Cerklje is also a starting point for climbing Krvavec, an Alpine skiing center.

At first the road leading from Preddvor through the picturesque valley of Kokra turns east. Under the ridge Kalški greben the valley turns north and then below the Grintovci extends into the Jezersko valley (880 m). A zigzag road leads from the valley to the Jezerski vrh mountain pass (1218) where is also an international border crossing with Austria. Jezersko is a popular tourist spot, as well.

Tržič

First ridges of the Karavanke chain can be made out behind the last peaks of the Kamnik-Savinja Alps. The old tradesmen town of Tržič grew over the centuries on the banks of the Kamniška Bistrica River between Dobrča and Kriška gora. It has been a town of shoemakers, leathersmiths and blacksmiths for ages. Numerous old houses with typical iron shutters are still preserved in the old town core, and the Tržič Museum is also worth visiting.

From Tržič a road leads up the Mošenik valley to the Ljubelj mountain pass (1369 m) in the Karavanke Chain and continues through a 1570 m long tunnel to Austria. On the Ljubelj lies the skiing center Zelenica. In Podljubelj there was a mercury mine until 1902. The nearby waterfall Tominčev slap is also worth seeing.

Behind Tržič, the Tržiška Bistrica valley turns northeast through the gorge Dolžanova soteska (with a geological study path) and through the scattered hamlet of Jelendol under the Košuta mountain ridge (2094).

The third valley starting in Tržič turns east behind the ridge of Kriška gora and brings us right under the north face of Storžič (2132 m). The road from Tržič to Begunje has one of the nicest views among Gorenjska roads.

Old town core of the craft town Tržič sits in a valley, squeezed among the steep slopes at the confluence of the Tržišku Bistrica and the Mošenik (top left). A walk through the old centre is educational and very interesting.

The Baroque Manor which houses the unique Museum of Apiculture , and the old parish church in Radovljica are built right above the Suha valley (top right).

From the edge of the Alpine plateau Jelovica extend great views of Dežela and the Karavanke (bottom). Although the Jelovica lies in the middle of tourist Gorenjska, it is quite possible to chance upon a bear in its forests. The plateau is also famous for the fact that you can easily get lost if you are not familiar with the territory.

Radovljica

Radovljica is situated on the last plain of the Ljubljana Basin, which the locals have named *Dežela* (the land). It is encompassed by woodlands in the south-east, and the Karavanke Chain and the Julian Alps with their high plateaus Jelovica, Pokljuka and Mežakla on other sides. There are two major valleys coming together at Radovljica: one is the blind valley of the Sava Bohinjka River which begins in the Bohinj basin, and the other is the Upper Sava Valley (Zgornja Savska dolina) which continues to Italy.

Radovljica is the center of *Dežela*. Its naturally well protected position on a promontory between the Sava and the Suha has played a very important role in its development. It acquired the status of a town in the 15th century. Even today there is a right-angled town square in the center, surrounded by old two-storey town houses. At one end of the square there is the parish church and the castle with a unique Museum of Apiculture. The most significant building in the old town core is the Šivec house, a tribute to the 16th century architecture, which today houses a gallery.

Lesce with its Aircraft Center has only developed after the arrival of the railway. In the Sava valley lies the popular bathing spot and camping site Šobec.

Begunje is a smaller village at the foot of the Karavanke in which you find Katzenstein Castle, used as a prison by the Germans during the WW II. Slovene patriots who were killed in the prison are buried in the surroundings and their graves are well tended. The former prison has been turned into a museum. Begunje is also known for the Avsenik Gallery. At the entrance into the Draga valley stand the ruins of Kamen Castle and atop the small hill above Begunje is St. Peter's Church which can easily be spotted from the valley as well. The Draga valley is the starting point for climbing Begunjščica (2063 m).

From Radovljica, one of the roads descends into the Sava valley leading to Lancovo, then continues via a saddle and further on through the Lipnica valley via Kamna gorica where a cluster of big houses reminds us that it is no peasant village.

Kropa is a picturesque village in the Kroparica ravine squeezed between steep slopes of the Jelovica plateau. Lack of demand for handmade ironwork at the end of the 19th century brought stagnation to the village and many people left. Kropa remained original, unchanged, old. It is a living museum of past times and worth visiting. The Blacksmith Museum in Kropa shows the history of iron mining and forging in Kropa and Kamna Gorica from the Middle Ages to the decline of iron industry.

Bled

Solitary hills jutting from the plain and surrounding Lake Bled are typical of the Bled area. The glacial lake fills a basin in the middle of glacial rubble and has a reputation of being extremely beautiful. It is adorned by the medieval castle perched on top of a high natural cliff-face and by an islet with a church.

The shore has been turned into a magnificent park with villages, hotels and villas. In the background of this paradise we can see forest-covered slopes of Jelovica with its rocky edge and the cliff Babji zob, and the Pokljuka plateau On a bright sunny day you can make out the white peaks of the Julian Alps, behind it.

Beginnings of tourism in Bled were modest. There was a wooden shed with thermal water used for bathing on the spot where today stands hotel the Toplice Hotel. In 1855, the Swiss doctor Arnold Rikli started treating its patients with sun, air and water. It was only after the construction of the railway that Bled developed into a mundane summer resort.

Today, Bled is a modern holiday resort with many hotels, private accommodation facilities, a camp site and a very rich culinary offer. It is also renowned as a rowing and regatta center, and as a starting point for numerous walks and tours. Almost in the center of Bled is Straža with ski slopes, and only 8 kilometers from Bled, on the slopes of the Pokljuka, lies Zatrnik with 19 km of skiing tracks. Only a bit further, on the Rudno polje clearing, there are skiing grounds for cross-country skiing and biathlon.

At the edge of the plain, in the triangle between the confluence of the two Savas, lie several villages: touristically developed Ribno, Bodešče, Koritno and Selo. On the north side lies Podhom, the starting point for one of the greatest natural sights near Bled, the picturesque Vintgar gorge, out carved by the Radovna River.

The poet dr. France Prešeren wrote: "Nowhere in the world is there a more lovely place, than this paradise and its suroundings". It would be hard to give a more accurate description of Bled in a simple sentence (top).

The Church of St. John the Baptist in Bohinj (bottom) stands above the efflux of the Sava Bohinjka River from the Lake Bohinj. The river flows out of the lake under a stone bridge. On the right side of the bridge is the tourist center of Bohinj, Ribčev Laz.

Bohinjska Bela lies at the mouth of the Sava Bohinjka valley under the steep slope of Pokljuka.

Bohinj

Bohinj is called the pearl of the Julian Alps. The whole of the Bohinj Basin and the lake especially, is encompassed by steep precipitous cliffs of the Julian Alps.

The largest settlement, Bohinjska Bistrica, has developed at the beginning of the basin. It is the administrative center of the Bohinj Basin. The tourist center of Bohinj, Ribčev Laz, is only a few kilometers away.

The 15th century Church of St. John makes part of the picturesque scenery around the lake. Its simple Ghotic architecture and wall paintings make it a prominent cultural and historical monument.

In the upper part of the va
lley there are several important villages like Stara Fužina with its old Alpine-styled houses, and Studor retaining its typical domestic atmosphere with famous double hay-racks *toplars*, scattered on the meadows near the village. There is also a Museum of Alpine diary farming.

From Stara Fužina leads a path to the magnificent Alpine valley Voje. Right from the beginning of the valley, from Devil's bridge (Hudičev most) we can see the picturesque gorge with the ravines cut by the Mostnica brook.

The whole Lake Bohinj lies within the Triglav National Park. The lake has been protected from construction of buildings on the shore thus it preserved its natural look. The water in the lake is extremely clear. Ukanc, backed by the mighty wall of Komarča, shuts off the Bohinj basin behind the lake.

The 3.5 km long Savica River, which springs out in the midst of the Komarča rocky wall and falls as the mighty Savica waterfall into the pool 71 meters lower, flows into lake Bohinj.

Vogel, rising 1000 m high above the lake, is reachable by a cable car leaving from Ukanc. There is a skiing resort on top of Vogel and another skiing grounds can be found almost in the center of Bohinj.

All that beautiful nature, peacefulness and unspoiled nature offer superb conditions for development of tourism and make Bohinj one of the most beautiful Alpine holiday resorts as well as an excellent starting point for shorter or longer walks around the Triglav National Park. Easier tours lead to Uskovica (1100 m) from the Voje , and on the Blato Alp (1142 m) above the Voje there are picturesque pastoral homesteads. Nearby is Vogar (1053 m) with excellent views. The starting point for a climbing tour to Komna, a large plateau in the heart of the Julian Alps, is by the Savica waterfall. Between two mountain ridges above Komarča, slightly arching in the direction of Kanjavec (2568 m) and Triglav (2864 m) lies the green Triglav Lakes Valley.

Žirovnica

In Žirovnica, situated at the foot of Stol (2236 m), the highest mountain in the Karavanke Chain, ends the plain of the Ljubljana Basin. In the direction of Begunje we find a number of villages: Doslovče, the birthplace of the writer Franc Finžgar, Breznica, the birthplace of the pioneer of Slovene apiculture Anton Janša, Vrba, the birthplace of the greatest Slovene poet France Prešeren and naturally Žirovnica, the hometown of Prešeren's mentor Matija Čop.

Up the Sava stretches the Upper Sava Valley (Zgornjesavska dolina). In Moste pri Žirovnici the Sava is dammed with the second highest dam in Slovenia. On the south bank of the dam lies the village of Blejska Dobrava, and on the north bank are Javornik and Koroška Bela which already make part of Jesenice.

Jesenice

Jesenice is an industrial town which until 1990 used to be almost completely dependent on the Jesenice Iron and Steel Works. The Technical Museum shows the history of iron industry in the valley. In the picturesque country between Jesenice and the Austrian border on the Karavanke ridges, at an altitude of 1000 m, lie villages Planina pod Dolico and Javorniški Rovt. The opposite side of the valley is shut off by the steep gloomy north slope of the Mežakla plateau.

On the Hrušica there is an international border crossing with Austria. There is an 8000 m long road tunnel leading through the Karavanke.

Meadows on Planina pod Golico are whitened by millions of blossoming daffodils every April (top left).
Jesenice is squeezed in the Sava Dolinka valley among the steep slopes of the Karavanke and the Mežakla plateau (bottom). Slovenia and Austria are linked by two 8 km long tunnels on Hrušica under Karavanke, through one leads the road and through the other the railroad.

The Sava Dolinka is trapped in the highest dam in Slovenia (over 50 meters) for the Žirovnica hydro power station (top). Its surface is 0.7 km2. On the left bank of the dam sits Koroška Bela, a Jesenice suburb, and on the right bank is the village of Blejska Dobrava a starting point for excursions to the Blejski Vintgar gorge.

Mojstrana

Higher up the Upper Sava Valley the Karavanke Chain lowers and high rocky ridges of the Julian Alps come into close vicinity of the valley. Three magnificent alpine valleys open from the Upper Sava Valley towards the main ridge of the Julian Alps: Vrata, Kot and Krma. At the very entrance into the Vrata lie alpine villages Mojstrana and Dovje. This 10 km long valley ends in a huge basin under the over 1000 m high Triglav North Face. Jakob Aljaž, a priest from Dovje, erected in 1895 at his expense the Aljaž tower right on top of Triglav (2864). In 1896 the Slovene Mountaineering Society built the mountain hut on Kredarica (2515) just under the pyramidal top of Triglav. Triglav, the highest Slovene mountain is of great importance to the Slovenes. It is also in their coat-of-arms. Another curiosity in the Vrata is the 52 m high Peričnik waterfall.

Further up the Upper Sava Valley lies, in the direction of the Julian Alps, the torrent gorge of the Beli potok, and in the direction of the Karavanke the gorges of the Belca and Mlinca brooks.

Kranjska gora

Gozd Martuljek is a picturesque tourist alpine village. The Hladnik brook, which springs in the Karavanke, runs through a narrow gorge and then through the village. Another brook running through the village is the Martuljek with its two waterfalls - Zgornji Martuljkov slap which is rather hard to access, and Spodnji Martuljkov slap with a clear and well marked trail leading to it.

Within a shooting range from Martuljek lies Kranjska gora with the Pišnica valley and its two side valleys Mala Pišnica and Krnica, opening south from it. A mountain road from the Pišnica leads to the picturesque Trenta valley over the highest mountain pass in Slovenia, the Vršič saddle (1611 m).

Kranjska gora is a well-known tourist center both for winter and summer sports. In winter it is a magnet for skiers, and in summer, with the clear lake Jasna in the picturesque Pišnica valley, for bathers. The area offers numerous possibilities for spending active holidays in nature.

For a number of years, Kranjska Gora has been host to World Cup competitions in alpine skiing. The ethnological museum in the Liznjek house is worth visiting as well.

Podkoren is a typical alpine village with old Alpine - styled houses. At Podkoren the road mounts towards the saddle Korensko sedlo (1073), an international border crossing with Austria. Right behind Podkoren lies the spring of the Sava Dolinka River - Zelenci.

Only 100 meters from Italian border sits Rateče, the last village before the border. In front of the village, atop a small hill, is a little walled church. Under Jalovec (2645 m) arguably the most beautiful mountain of Julian Alps lies the glacial Tamar valley. Planica is world famous for its ski jumps, among which is also the one intended for ski-flying where bold ski-jumpers fly over 200 meters far.

Mojstrana has a magnificent view of the very heart of the mountains (top). From this Alpine village lead three mighty valleys: Vrata, Krma and a slightly less known Kot. Through the Vrata runs a 12 km long road which leads via the Peričnik waterfalls to the mountain hut Aljažev dom in the Vrata. There is only a short walk from the hut to the foot of the mighty, over 1000 metres high, Triglav North Face (middle right).

Kranjska gora (bottom right) is a well known skiing resort. It is also host to World Cup competitions in alpine skiing. Summer tourism is taking off as well.

Only a few kilometers away is Planica. Is there anyone who hasn't yet heard of the valley under Ponce whose ski jumps are famous far beyond Slovene borders?

Škofja Loka

Sharp ridge of Lubnik (1025 m) changes into a steep slope and continues for almost 700 m down to the Selška Sora River, and on the other side with a bit lees steep slope to the Poljanska Sora River. Towards the east it passes into rounded hills and descends over a terrace to the confluence of the two Soras. On the gravel and on the terrace lies the old town core of Škofja Loka. A big castle is perched above the town.

Škofja Loka was founded in 973 by the bishops of Freising who ruled the town for 830 years, until 1803 when the territory was nationalized by the Austrian Emperor. The town was ruined by an earthquake in 1511, rebuilt later on and has remained practically unchanged until today. Škofja Loka has the best preserved town center with a castle in Slovenia. The castle houses the Town Museum.

Cultural and entertaining events have a long tradition in Škofja Loka. Over the summer numerous concerts take place in the ancient ambiance of Mestni trg, while the castle houses exhibitions. There is also a fair every Wednesday in the former barracks. And weddings are quite common as well (right).

Crngrob, situated at the foot of Kovk (584) between Škofja Loka and Kranj, is known for its church with 13th century Romanesque parts of the building and 15th century wall paintings.

The valley Poljanska dolina, separating the Škofja Loka Hills and the Polhov Gradec Dolomites, begins at Škofja Loka. The Škofja Loka Hills stretch west from Lubnik in a long ridge, composed of Stari vrh (1217) with a ski center, Koprivnik (1939), Blegoš (1562) and Črni vrh above Cerkno. Northern part of the Škofja Loka Hills is separated from the Jelovica by the valley Selška dolina.

If you just drive through the Selška dolina valley you will never feel it. The Selška dolina (middle right) can only be experienced when you take hidden but well kept roads and drive through side gorges and up the steep slopes of green hills. Ridges of the hills are scattered with small villages and solitary farms, whose inhabitants are vigorous and hospitable. First farmhouses which opened their doors to visitors were right here, on Čretna raven under Stari vrh, on the ridge separating the Selška and Poljanska dolina valleys.

Poljanska dolina

The lower part of the Poljanska dolina valley has been settled as early as the 13th and 14th centuries. Visoko boasts a castle and the vault of the Slovene writer Ivan Tavčar. Important villages in the valley are Poljane and Gorenja vas. From Poljane leads a forest road via Javorje and Žetina almost to the top of Blegoš.

At Gorenja vas the valley extends and splits - the Poljanska dolina turns straight to the west, while the narrow Brebovščica valley cuts into the Polhov

High in the hills, under the rocky walls of Ratitovec, lies Sorica (bottom right). It is the birthplace of the impressionist painter Ivan Grohar (1867-1911). In his house there is a small museum and visitors can participate in workshops on music and painting.

Old preserved town core in Škofja Loka (left) is squeezed on the terrace under the mighty castle.

Gradec Dolomites. The road through it takes you via Lučine to Horjul.

At Hotavlje, known for its marble, the valley turns southwest. Between Stara Oselica and Koprivnik leads the road through the narrow Hobovščica ravine via Sovodenj and Kladje pass (787 m) to Cerkno.

From Fužine, where they forged nails already in the 16th century, leads a road, hewed into the hill above the Sora, through a narrow ravine to the small Žiri basin. Old farming villages of Selo, Dobračevo, Stara vas, Nova vas and Žiri joined, forming a friendly small town of Žiri. From Žiri there is one road leading via Razpotje (709 m) to Idrija and another one going up the Upper Sora Valley via Rovte to Logatec.

Selška dolina

The valley Selška dolina is more of a mountain valley. It has several small valleys stretching from it to both sides. In the valley we find the settlements of Praprotno, Bukovica, Ševlje, Dolenja vas, Selca and a larger town, Železniki. Železniki was founded in the 14th century by the Friuli blacksmiths following the order of the bishops of Freising. In the 17th century 2000 people were working in the iron industry in Železniki. Last furnace was extinguished in 1901.

The last settlement in the valley is Zali Log from which leads the road via the pass Petrovo Brdo (803 m) and through the gorge Baška grapa to the Tolminsko region. To the north, a road leads through the village of Sorica (821 m), settled already in the 13th century, and over the pasture Soriška planina (1277 m), which is a skiing center, to Bohinj. On the southern slopes above the valley we find a number of isolated mountain farms. They make part of Davča village, superficially the largest Slovene village.

Primorska, the Kras and the Gorica region

This region is a world of its own. It is the most varied Slovene territory: it covers wild alpine world, high snow-capped rocky peaks, deep wild valleys, the karst world with famous caves and other karst phenomena, and the blue Adriatic sea. This is a country of mild Mediterranean and harsh Alpine climates, of noble Lipizzaners, mysterious underground and a hymn to the mountains.

A holiday or an excursion to the seaside, to the Kras, the land of *pršut* and Teran, or to the wild Soča Valley can be so thrilling and joyful that it is always a pleasure to return.

The Trenta Valley

It is from the Vršič saddle, the highest mountain pass in Slovenia, that we can first enjoy the magnificent view of the wild mountain ridges stretching to the south. Deep under the steep, mainly precipitous cliffs, winds the Trenta Valley, the valley that the famous mountaineer dr. Julius Kugy (1858 - 1944) loved so passionately and described so poetically in his works.

The upper, blind part of the valley is called Zadnja Trenta. Scattered all over the valley are typical isolated Trenta homesteads. Trenta is from all sides encompassed by mighty mountains: Mojstrovka (2366 m), Jalovec (2654 m) Prisojnik (2547 m), Razor (2601 m), Planja (2453 m), Goličica (2101 m), Trentarski Pelc (2109 m) and rocky ridge of Veliki Pelc (2388 m).

Under the steep slope of mighty Mojstrovka lies the source of the Soča River (916 m), arguably the most beautiful European river, flowing over gravel down through the narrow valley, sparkling and crystal clear. From the amphitheater surrounded by Prisojnik, Razor, Planja and Goličica springs the Mlinarica, which right before it throws itself into the Soča runs trough a wild gorge.

Wilderness of the Trenta, mysterious gorges, unspoiled nature of the Triglav National Park and arguably the most beautiful European river, the Soča (top), leave a visitor with an indelible impression. Particular to this clean green river is the Soča trout which grows to unimaginable sizes. It is not so uncommon that a Soča fisherman can boast with a meter long trout. It is also one of the reasons that make people from far and near return to the magic embrace of the river.

On solitary farmhouses (bottom), among the steep slopes of the valley, life was no bed of roses. Today the majority of the idyllic farmhouses are actually weekend-cottages and people from the valley found in tourism an easier way to survive. But due to the harsh weather conditions the tourist season in the Trenta is limited to the warmest summer time. And even then, mornings are quite fresh, far from expected.

The tunnel leading from Log pod Mangrtom (middle) to Italy was made as early as 1903 because of the needs of the lead mine in Rabelj. And high above the valley, Mangart (2679 m) rises steeply to the sky.

From the side valley of Zadnjica a bit further down the Soča, flows the Zadnjica brook. At the confluence of the Soča and the Zadnjica lies the village of Na Logu, the first clustered settlement in the valley and the center of the Trenta where we can find the Trenta Museum. Nearby is the Alpine botanical garden Juliana, designed and set up a century ago by dr. Julius Kugy.

Through the valley of Spodnja Trenta the road along the Soča brings us to the village of Soča overlooking the Lepena valley in the south-east. From the Lepena valley lead mountain trails past the Krn and the Komna to Bohinj. Those parts are perfect for long and exciting mountain trips.

Behind the village of Soča the valley turns west. After the last narrows between Svinjak (1637 m) and Javoršček (1549 m) the valley widens into the Bovec basin.

Although there is only 80 km of air distance between the Soča source and its outfall into the Adriatic sea the landscape is impossibly picturesque and varied. On its short journey, Soča is greeted by deep alpine valleys, green mountain pastures, karst plateaus and the Italian Friuli plain.

Under Mangart

North of the Bovec basin between Svinjak and Rombon (2208 m) lies the Koritnica valley. Under the Kluže fortification lies the famous up to 60 m deep Koritnica gorge with its ravines. The road leads through the gorge, which used to be protected by the fortress, to Log pod Mangrtom, one of the most beautiful Slovene villages, and to the Predel mountain pass (1156 m) which is also an international border crossing with Italy. About a kilometer before the border, a road branches off and turns steeply up the slope, bringing us to the saddle Mangartsko sedlo (2072) right under the top of Mangart. It is the highest road in Slovenia. The saddle offers great views of the Julian Alps and the Koritnica valley, lying 1110 m under an overhang cliff.

Bovec

The Bovec basin is a depression among the mountains. During the Ice Age glaciers filled it with enormous amounts of rubble. For a long time it was filled with water. The Polovnik ridge (1471 m) shuts it off from the south and the Kanin ridge (2587 m) from the north. Kanin boasts the highest ski center in Slovenia. Bovec developed on the high terrace above the Soča. During the World War I it was completely destroyed.

Today Bovec represents the economic center of the upper part of the Soča Valley. It is a small, fast growing tourist town surrounded with natural beauties offering a number of possibilities for active holidaying in every season. The number of visitors is constantly growing.

The Boka River springs from the Kanin slope and as a mighty 30 meters wide waterfall immediately drops for 106 m. After a kilometer of torrential current it flows into the Soča. Soon after the confluence the Soča winds around the Polovnik ridge.

The road splits at Žaga. One fork leads through the Učeja valley to the nearby border crossing with Italy and the other among steep wooded slopes through the Soča Valley to the southeast. Trnovo ob Soči is a well-known kayak center. Alpine architecture in this village already shows a strong Mediterranean influence.

Krn (2244 m)

Above the Zatolmin valley is a wooden church, Javorca, (top right) a WW I memorial.

The Soča is trapped into a big dam at Most na Soči (middle right).

Not many people go swimming in the Soča but fishermen, kayak paddlers and rafts can be seen daily (bottom right).

Kobarid

Between Trnovo and Kobarid the Soča runs through a deep gorge. On the east bank is a terraced world with several villages. Behind them rises the 800 m high west wall of Krn (2245 m). Krn is the last Julian mountain with a height over 2000 m along the Soča short stream and a bloody fortification from the World War I.

The Kobarid Museum collection is dedicated to the Isonzo front, while the Italian Ossuary *(Kostnica)* in Kobarid and military cemetaries scattered all over Zgornje Posočje bear witness to the victims of the Isonzo front. At Kobarid (234 m) the valley Staroselska dolina with several nice villages branches off west from the Soča Valley. The road through the valley leads towards the village of Robič and further on to the border crossing with Italy.

From Staro selo up the Nadiža valley, the road leads via the village of Borjana, half of which was in 1952 buried under an avalanche from the slope of Kobariški stol, to Breginj (550 m), almost completely destroyed by the

Javorca

Tolmin

The Soča Valley widens at Tolmin. The Soča makes a big meander around Bučenica (510 m) and Mrzli vrh (590 m), while the road towards Nova Gorica leads through a dry valley and the village of Volče. Near Tolmin the Soča is joined by the Tolminka, and a bit further downstream, at Most na Soči, by the Idrijca. In the gorge between Kuk (638 m) and Mrzli vrh under Selo pri Volčah the Soča is dammed, making thus a 42 hectares large and 32 m deep dam in Most na Soči.

Tolmin is situated on a high terrace between the Soča and the Tolminka rivers. An excellent defence position was even more protected by the Kozlov rob hill (426 m) above the town atop which the Patriarchs of Aquileia built a fortified castle. They were succeeded by the Counts of Gorizia for a while. A silent witness to the severe fighting during the WW I is the German Ossuary, while the Tolmin Museum exhibits archeological and ethnological collections.

Among the steep slopes north of Tolmin lies the Tolminka gorge with its 60 m deep ravines *(Tolminska korita)*. The road above them leads to the glacial valley Zatolmin.

Poljubinj lies on a terrace west of Tolmin. A bit further down is Prapetno with a valley stretching west to Kneža. Further south, on the very shore of the dam, sits Modrej. Most na Soči is built on a rocky promontory at the confluence of the Soča and the Idrijca rivers. The St. Maver's Church in Most na Soči is mentioned in 1192 pontifical bull. Touristically, the town has been developing fast during the last decade.

1976 earthquake. The south slope of Kobariški stol rises above the villages and its ridge stretches far west into Venetia. There are two other villages in the surroundings which, on the other hand, managed to preserve their old cores: Logje and Robidišče.

From Kobarid on, the Soča still flows over snow white gravel. It is clean and characteristically green, sometimes blue. It flows through a kilometer wide fertile valley which shows a strong influence of Mediterranean climate.

The Baška grapa Valley

The Baška grapa Valley is like a gully cut into the rocks. The bottom of the valley is crisscrossed by the tiny Bača, the road and the rail which passes through numerous tunnels. Squeezed in the gorge are the small villages of Klavže, Krteža, Grahovo, Koritnica, Huda Južna and Podbrdo. At Podbrdo the railroad enters the Bohinj tunnel while the main road via the Petrovo Brdo pass leads to Selška dolina.

At Kneža, the deep Kneža valley cuts deep into the mountains. A forest road leads right under the very peak of Šije (1880 m) on Bohinj Vogel. Southern part of the Baška grapa is at first shut off by Šentvid plateau (Šentviška planota), by Kojca (1303 m) and by Porezen (1630 m), separating the Baška grapa from the Idrijca valley.

Cerkno

The whole Idrija-Cerkno region is a vast wooded prae-Alpine world with deep valleys and extremely steep slopes. Individual small settlements and solitary mountain farms are scattered right up to the ridges and peaks.

Two valleys begin at Dolenja Trebuša - the Trebuščica valley and the Hotenja valley. These are lonely and scarcely settled areas with numerous steep and hardly accessible ravines. The Cerknica flows into the Idrijca at Želin, while the Cerknica valley stretches right to the foot of Porezen. This is where Cerkno lies. Originally the settlement was an ecclesiastic center. The most famous monument in the Cerkno valley is the Franja Partisan Hospital dating from the WW II, hidden in a ravine by the Pasica stream above the village of Log. Above Novaki lies a well known ski center Črni Vrh (1291 m). In the village of Ravne above Cerkno is the Raven cave (Ravenska jama) known for the snow white aragonite crystals resembling ice, needles and even hedgehogs (aragonitni ježki).

From Cerkno, a road leads up via Planina pri Cerknem and after the Kladje pass (787 m) descends to the Poljanska dolina.

At Mardi Gras, Laufarji fill the streets of Cerkno (top left). There is a number of other interesting old masks in the carnival. This rich tradition has also been preserved in some other villages in the area. All masks gather for the traditional Mardi Gras promenade in Cerkno.

In the whole Idrija-Cerkno region villages are perched on the steep slopes above the valleys (top right). Life wasn't easy here either, but now tourism is developing fast. Traffic has been banned from the whole area of the Zgornja Idrijca Regional Park. The Klavže and barriers are still preserved there as well as the water filled rake used for transporting wood to the valley. Wood was used by the mercury mine in Idrija. Right at the beginning of the park, under a mighty rocky wall, is Wild Lake. The picturesque surroundings of the lake from which springs a small river, are known for a number of botanical curiosities.

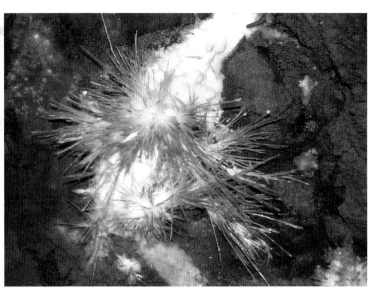

One of the most important natural sights in the Idrija-Cerkno Hills is the Raven cave. Entrance into the cave is near the first houses of Ravne pri Cerknem. The ceiling of otherwise mediocre cave is sprinkled with aragonite crystals (top right). They can be found in other caves, too, but in none of them so beautiful, so numerous and so easily accessible.

People from Cerkno also like to boast with a unique archaeological find in Europe, a prehistoric wind instrument unearthed in the Divje Babe cave. A visit to the Anthony mine shaft in the Idrija mercury mine might also turn out very interesting. The entrance to the shaft is in the center of Idrija.

Idrija

The narrow valley first widens at Spodnja Idrija. Among the Idrija Hills to the west of Spodnja Idrija lies the narrow Kadomljica valley. The road through it leads via the Oblakov vrh pass (721 m) to the Hotenje valley. At Mokraška vas between Spodnja Idrija and Idrija a narrow zigzag road leading to Žiri branches off into the steep slope.

Idrija has completely filled the small basin under steep wooded slopes. The town was founded after the discovery of mercury (živo srebro) the 15th century. For centuries, Idrija mine gave the purest mercury in the world. Today the mine is closed, but it can be visited by tourists. The Municipal Museum is housed in the Gewerkeneg castle, purpose-built for the mine administration and storage of mercury in 1533. Idrija's greatest natural sight is Wild Lake (Divje jezero), a deep clear lake situated under a 100 m high overhang wall under the Zadlog and Idrijski Log plateaus. Since 1972 Wild Lake has been considered a natural museum. It lies on the fringe of the Zgornja Idrijca Regional Park.

Idrija, which used to be a wealthy town due to the mercury mine, is after its closure fast turning to tourism.

The Goriška Brda

A road from Plave leads up a steep hill. Vrhovlje offers a view of hilly wine region Goriška Brda. Another road to that region comes from Solkan. Although the Goriška Brda is like a tongue stretching into Italy, the villages in the region are completely Slovene. It is interesting that the villages at the foot of Brda on the Italian side are Italian. National border is very clear here. The Goriška Brda is known for excellent wines and numerous wine cellars.

Ruins on the hill testify to the fact that Kojsko used to be a fortified village. Nearby are villages Šmartno and Vedrijan. At Dobrovo is a restored castle and a big wine cellar where most of the wine from the Brda is brought. At the southernmost end of the Brda lies Vipolže, known for its Renaissance castle and a 500 years old cypress alley.

Nova Gorica

After flowing through a narrow gorge between Sabotin (609 m) and Sveta Gora (681 m), the Soča leaves the mountains and enters the Friuli plain. It crosses the Slovene - Italian border at Solkan and runs on Italian territory until it flows into the Adriatic sea.

Solkan sits under Sabotin (609 m). In Roman times it was a military post which gave Solkan its name. Today Solkan is an integral part of Nova Gorica. Above Solkan lies the village of Grgar with a road passing through the Čepovan Valley (Čepovanska dolina) to the Idrijca valley.

Nova Gorica was only built after the WW II when Gorizia was awarded to Italy. The state border between Gorizia and Nova Gorica runs along the railroad in the middle of the two towns.

The Kromberk Castle was built in the 17th century and now houses the Gorica Museum.

There is a border crossing with Italy at Šempeter and another one only 3 km south, at Vrtojba.

Roads from four different directions and railroads from three meet in Dornberk. The railroad and the road to

The road crosses the bridge which is known for bungee jumping, and leads to the Goriška Brda. The railroad runs across the bridge up the Soča valley and then through the narrow Baška grapa and a tunnel to Bohinj and further on to Jesenice.

Grgar (right) is almost shyly hidden in a small basin. Its karst surroundings and ravines on the "intermittent" Slatna river are certainly worth seeing.

Numerous pilgrims drive to Sveta gora (681 m) above Solkan where you'll find a monastery with a big church. From the top of the mountain extend great views of the surrounding hills and the Gorica region, as well as across the Friouli Plain and all the way to the Adriatic sea.

Sežana are built in the narrow Branik Valley (Braniška dolina). In the wider part of the valley lies the village of Branik. On the hill above it sits Rihemberk Castle.

Vipava Valley

The Vipava Valley (Vipavska dolina) stretches between steep slopes of Trnovski gozd and the Nanos in the north, and hills at the foot of the Kras in the south. It consists of the valley bottom and of wine-growing hills.

The center of Vipava Valley is Ajdovščina, a crossroads of important roads leading through the valley: through Trnovski gozd to Lokve and the Idrijca valley, and from Gorizia to Postojna and Logatec. It was the site of walled Roman military camp with towers, called Castra ad Fluvium Frigidum ("the camp by the cold river" - the cold river being today's Hubelj). For centuries Ajdovščina has been in the possession of various aristocratic families. Due to its position it became the center of the Vipava Valley in the 18th century.

Written sources mention Vipavski križ as early as 1252. It was in its prime around 1500. At that time it was a walled town protected by a mighty Renaissance castle with four towers. The medieval core of the village is still preserved. There was also a monastery founded in 1636. In the 19th century, as Ajdovščina started to progress, the population of Vipavski Križ started to decline. At the end of the 19th century, a once mighty medieval town became and remained a village.

Another important town in the valley is Vipava. The Vipava River springs from a rocky wall in the old part of the town. Ruins of a castle are still visible on the rock. Near Vipava, in the direction of Ajdovščina, is atop a small hill Zemono Mansion surrounded by vineyards.

The villages in the Vipava Valley are situated among the vineyards on the slopes and hills. In winter those parts are hit by the bora (burja), northerly wind blowing from Trnovski gozd with a speed of over 150 km/h.

The Kras

The Kras consists of a limestone plateau with numerous dry valleys, potholes and karst caves, stretching between the Vipava Valley and the Gulf of Trieste. Here we can follow the underground stream of the Reka River flowing through the magnificent Škocjan caves system (Škocjanske jame). We also come across the Reka river over 200 m underground in the Kačna cave (Kačna jama) near Divača. After that the Reka River disappears in the mysterious underground and resurfaces again as the Timav in the Gulf of Trieste. Two other well known caves are Vilenica near Lokve and a more demanding Lipica cave (Lipiška jama) between Sežana and Lipica. The famous Lipizzaners, white horses of the Spanish riding school at the Vienna court, originate in the stud house in green Lipica. In the barren karst soil also grows the vine that gives the famous ruby-red wine Teran.

Sežana

The town was built by the road and the railroad to Trieste. It only started to progress after the WW II. Border crossing with Italy, Fernetiči (Fernetto), is only a kilometer from the town center.

One of the roads leads through the Senadal valley to Divača and Senožeče; the former is an important railway crossroads (lines Ljubljana - Koper and Trieste - Pulj).

A wine road leads from Sežana to the land of Teran. The old Kras village of Tomaj sits on a hill with a gorgeous view of the picturesque surroundings. Vineyards and small oak forests spread all around it on brown-red karst soil. Not far away is the village of Dutovlje. Above the Branik Valley, on Turn (363 m) sits an ancient walled village of Štanjel dating from the Middle Ages. On the top of the hill are ruins of the old defence tower from the 12th century and under it, in the clustered settlement around it, the 16th century castle of the Counts of Gorizia.

South of Sežana lies Lipica. The stud farm was established by the Vienna

The tradition of breeding noble white Lipizzaners goes back over 400 years (top right). The large grounds of the Lipica stud farm are surrounded by oak groves.

The karst villages of Tomaj and Dutovlje are the home of kraški Teran, a noble wine marked by the red karst soil and dry climate. Here wine cellars and good local inns are linked by a wine road.

In those parts, old collapsing karst houses are actually hard to come across nowadays (middle right). People became aware of the values of traditional architecture and the number of houses with fenced yards rebuilt in traditional style increases.

Štanjel looks down on the karst landscape from the top of a hill. It is a true medieval town with a castle and mighty town walls. Houses are old and built of stone. Some of them are still lived in and some have been demolished or there are only stone walls jutting out. Despite that, a walk through this ancient town is worth a couple of hours of your precious time.

court in 1580. Lippizzaners were bred from local and Spanish breeds. The stud farm (kobilarna) lies in a green oasis in the middle of barren karst. It is surrounded by a forest of centennial oak trees. Only a kilometer away lies the Lipica border crossing with Italy.

Kozina

The Materija valley (Matarsko podolje) stretches between the Brkini Hills and the Čičarija Range further down from Slavnik (1028 m), the last peak in Primorska that rises above 1000 m. The Podgorski kras plateau under Slavnik gradually descends to Istria. Numerous streams flowing from the Brkini slopes disappear underground when they meet with karst soil. At the edge of the karst plateau each stream has cut a blind valley surrounded by rocky cliffs from three sides. The area abounds in pits and caves The most famous cave system is Dimnice near Markovščina which is also open to tourists.

The road linking Rijeka and Trieste through the Materija valley was already very important in Roman times.

From Hrpelje pri Kozini leads a forest road to the top of Slavnik.

A road leads from Dobrovo to the Čičarija range, most of which lies in Croatia. Golac is the only Slovene village in the Čičarija range.

Podgorski kras descends with crags and scraps into the Rižana valley. On the edge of the plateau above Trieste, right next to the border with Italy, is the Socerb fortress with a beautiful view of Trieste and its surroundings.

Istria

From the road leading to the coast extends a superb vista of the hilly country and the sea. Clustered small villages are scattered over rounded ridges so that they resemble small towns. Steep slopes of numerous valleys are covered with impenetrable forests. Ridges stretch into the sea forming a picturesque jagged coastline.

This is the warmest part of Slovenia. Winters are usually mild with temperatures hardly ever dropping below 0°C. A road branches off from the main road under Črni Kal and leads to the Osapska reka valley. Galjevica lies by the road to Osp. The village of Osp sits under a large overhang cliff under which lies a cave with the spring of the Osapska reka River.

On the west side of the valley rises Tinjan (374 m) with an extraordinary view of Primorska. The main road leads from Črni Kal to the Rižana valley. In the upper part of the valley lies Hrastovlje with a 12th century pilgrimage church. Inside the church is the famous Dance of Death fresco from 1490. In the 16th century the church was fortified with a high wall.

South from the Rižana valley the road zigzags up the once fortified Kubed hill and descends into the fertile valley, bringing us to a border crossing with Croatia near Buzet.

Above the valley lies a picturesque dry and fertile valley called Moravška vala. To the west, all the way to the Dragonja valley and further down to the sea, stretch hills and ridges scattered with stone built villages, which are so typical of the area.

The rock walls above Osp (top) are suitable for free-climbing. Free-climbers come here even in winter since it has mild Mediterranean climate without snow, ice and low temperatures.

Fig and olive trees (top right) are typical of the region.

Portorož (middle right) is the main Slovene seaside resort. Long sandy beach is packed in the summer.

Ancient narrow Mediterranean streets are very appealing in the summer heat, and in winter, when bora howls mercilessly over the roofs, they offer shelter. The narrow streets of Koper (bottom right) are also full of strolling people.

Ankaran

Ankaran is a small seaside resort stretching along the southern part of the Milje Peninsula (Miljski polotok) on top of which in the east-west direction runs the border between Slovenia and Italy.

Ankaran was inhabited as early as the Antique. The 11th century Benedictine monastery was first turned into a summer residence in the 18th century, and then into a hotel in 1922. Ankaran is a nice town full of lush Mediterranean flora with a kilometer long sandy beach.

Atop the 150 m high rounded ridge of the Milje peninsula sits a larger village, Hrvatini, and several smaller settlements.

Koper

Koper's Old Town was built on an island which was joined to the mainland by a causeway in the 19th century. Draining of the marshy area between the island and mainland left behind the plain on which later developed the trade and industrial center of Koper.

The Romans called Koper the Goat island *(Insula Caprea)*. Since the 13th century Koper was under the jurisdiction of the Venetian Republic. During the Middle Ages it became the administrative and judicial center for Istria. There were as many as five Koper mayors on the throne of Venetian doges. Medieval town was surrounded by strong walls with 12 gates. The main gate still stands.

Among rich medieval town houses and palaces were also a few monasteries. Many buildings from the period between the 15th and 18th centuries are still preserved and even today give the town a magnificent look. Some of the most important buildings are: the Praetorian Palace (Pretorska palača) from the 15th century, the Cathedral in Ghotic and Renaissance style with rich Baroque interior from the 15th and 16th centuries, the Garvisi Palace, the Carpaccio house, the Tocco Palace housing the ethnographic museum and an archeological collection, etc.

After the WW II Koper changed drastically and modernized. On the slope of Markovec (223 m) developed a residential area called Semedela. Today Koper is also Slovenia's only shipping port.

Izola

The road passing from Koper under steep, occasionally hewn, slopes brings us to old fishing port of Izola. The old part of Izola sits on a small limestone peninsula stretching into the sea from a smaller plain where we find new part of the town. Together with the Livada and Jagodje districts they are part of Izola.

In the 2nd century the Romans built here *Haliaetum*. The town was construed by the refugees from Aquileia. Izola came under Venetian jurisdiction together with Koper. From the Belvedere hill offering a great view of Izola, the road descends into the Strunjan Bay through an avenue of stone pine trees.

Piran

Piran, a town of narrow steep streets and a large main square, sits at the very tip of a narrow peninsula stretching into the sea from the Šavrinska brda Hills.

Piran has been settled since the Illyrian times and came under Venetian jurisdiction at the same time as Koper and Izola, in 1283. Even at that time Piran was fortified by strong walls with guard towers on the mainland part. The main city gate in the town walls still stands.

Piran parish church, which was built in the 17th century, dominates above the town. A number of Ghotic and Baroque palaces testify to the economic power that Piran used to have.

Today, Piran is a typical Mediterranean coast town with a well

The old town core of Izola was built on a peninsula. The fishing port (top) is the busiest early in the morning when numerous boats return from fishing.

The medieval town core of Piran (top right) is practically inaccessible by car. A labyrinth of narrow streets and passages, in places so narrow that two people can hardly pass, is lined with medieval stone houses.

There are practically no limitations for nudists in Slovenia. You can come across them in more or less hidden corners all along the coast (middle right), as well as along the rivers on lake shores. They are no longer a rarity that would shock old ladies.

Although Slovene coast has no islands, there is a number of tourist boats offering rides (bottom right). There is also plenty of moorings for sailing boats and motor boats on the Slovene coast. Beside the moorings in the ports there are also three marines in Koper, Izola and Piran. But there are also other interesting sights. Very interesting is also the Piran Aquarium where we can see the fauna typical of the Slovene sea.

preserved old core. In the summer heat, the cool of its narrow streets and its rich history attract masses of tourists.

Portorož

Tourism began to develop in Portorož at the end of the 19th century. Today Portorož, together with Lucija, is a an attractive, well-known holiday resort with a big marina, numerous hotels, a Forma Viva on the small peninsula between Seča and Lucija and a kilometer of sandy beaches.

The Sečovlje plain was washed down by the Dragonja. In the plain lie the abandoned salt pans. Near Sečovlje is also an aircraft center.

Notranjska

Notranjska hides in its bosom an underground kingdom, an immense labyrinth of pits, caves, tunnels and streams hidden from everyday visitors and observers. Underground flow through unknown and only partly discovered tunnels veritable rivers, forming magnificent waterfalls, countless rapids and true lakes. It is a magnificent world, especially in places where water has hollowed out big halls into limestone layers. In complete darkens, millions of stalactites of breathtaking shapes and colours have been formed. Beauties of the Notranjska underground have since long been a magnet for visitors.

There is no other place anywhere in the world that could match Notranjska. Subterranean streams regularly resurfacing and singing their brief greeting to the sun soon again disappear into the darkness of the underground world. Spring and autumn rains fill up the famous intermittent lakes. In all this unspoiled nature a visitor finds himself surprised by the rich history of the province.

Logatec

The Logatec basin resembles a karst polje. The northern part of the valley is called Pusto polje and has no water but plenty of potholes and coniferous forests. Through the southern part of the valley runs the Logaščica stream which disappears underground practically in the center of Logatec. In Roman times it was a military camp.

The town later developed from seven villages and lived off the transport trade for centuries.

Near Logatec the old road linking Ljubljana and Koper is joined by the main road from Idrija and Ajdovščina. The road along Pusto polje leads to Žiri and the Poljanska dolina.

Planinsko polje

The old road leads through Grčarevec along the edge of the Planinsko polje,

Vast meadows of Lake Cerknica are filled with water in rainy periods. Its surface is then up to 24 km2. When the water starts disappearing, numerous streams wind like snakes across the field, and you can also see the swallowholes through which the water flows underground. One of the larger swallowholes is Rešeto near Dolenja vas pri Cerknici (top). The water also disappears underground through numerous subterranean caves. It resurfaces again in the Rakov Škocjan, but the Rak River is only 2 km long before it disappears underground again. In the dark shafts of the Planina cave the Rak joins the Pivka River which comes from the Postojna cave. After the confluence the river is called Unica and it resurfaces again in the Planinsko polje (bottom right). At the other end of the polje it disappears again and resurfaces near Vrhnika as the Ljubljanica.

the most typical karst polje in Slovenia. Planinsko polje stretches between Zagora and the Ravnik karst plateau. Planinsko polje is covered with meadows and scarce trees, it is only along the banks of the Unica river that

vegetation is denser. The Unica river bed is shalow and very meandering polje which makes it several times longer than the polje. Since the Unica floods the polje nearly every year, the villages are situated on the slopes surrounding the polje.

The Unica springs out from the Planina cave (Planinska jama) at the southernmost point of the polje. A path leading to the confluence of the Pivka and Rak is made through the cave. From the confluence on the river is called Unica. On a hill near the cave entrance is the Little Castle (Mali grad) which belonged to the Raubar aristocratic family. Further down the Unica are the ruins of the early Baroque Habsberg castle which was burnt down in the WW II. On the wooded hill above it are the ruins of another old castle. All those castles used to guard the important passage into the Postojna Gate.

Rakov Škocjan

Thick forests under Javornik hide a pearl - the Rakov Škocjan valley, also called the Rak valley. Ceilings of underground caves have collapsed and today the Rak runs in broad daylight. At both ends of the valley. parts of the ceilings were preserved, thus making two wonderful bridges - Mali naravni most at the eastern end and Veliki naravni most at the western end of the valley. The Rak flows in from Cerkniško polje through a cave under Nesrečni grič hill (712 m).

Lake Cerknica

The largest Slovene karst polje is Cerkniško polje or Lake Cerknica. It is the largest European intermittent lake with a surface of 24 km2. During rainy periods in the autumn and spring, when numerous springs from the edge of the polje and underground streams collecting water under the surrounding plateaus, rush into the polje, and the sinkholes and siphons cannot handle the outflow, then the polje usually becomes Lake Cerknica. In dry months the lake usually disappears.

Cerknica

Villages sit along the edge of the Cerkniško polje. The center of this part of Notranjska is Cerknica situated by the Cerkniščica stream under Slivnica (1114 m) which has superb views. It was a parish seat as early as the 13th century.

Between Menišija and Slivnica stretches the Cerkniščica valley with its numerous tributaries and side valleys. In a small basin sits the village of Begunje through which passes a road to the Rakitna plateau. Over the last decades Rakitna developed into a veritable holiday village.

The Lož Valley

To the northeast stretches the hilly world of the Bloke plateau (Bloška planota) scattered with villages and settlements. The village of Bloke is famous because its inhabitants made their own skis centuries ago.

The road from Cerknica to the Lož Valley (Loška dolina) passes the Križna cave (Križna jama) which has 22 underground lakes!

Through the valley flows the Obrh River which springs at two different places - under the Racna gora with the highest peak Petelinjek (1212 m) and under Snežnik (1796 m).

Lož, the first settlement in the valley was known already in the Middle Ages. It was granted a town charter in the 15th century. Atop the hill above Lož (698 m) lie ruins of Pusti Castle (Pusti grad). After the WW II Lož lost its town status and the primacy in the valley was taken by Stari trg pri Ložu.

Snežnik Castle sits near Kozarišče and is one of the most picturesque Slovene castles. It was first mentioned in writing 1268 as Sneperch. At that time it was in the possession of the Patriarchs of Aquileia who later presented it to the Lambergs. The building as it stands today dates from the 16th century and is built on a big rock surrounded by a natural water-filled gully. It houses a museum.

Snežnik Castle was built on a rock in the middle of a lake (top). It is one of the best preserved castles in Slovenia.

In a hidden valley, in the middle of a 123m high rocky cliff, is the never taken Predjama Castle (middle right). This most picturesque Slovene castle is connected with the legend of the rebelling baron Erazem Predjamski. Under the castle is an entrance into the mysterious underground world.

The Pivka river simply disappears into a hill (bottom right) in which is the Postojna cave. Here we can enter an almost 20 km long system of shafts, caves, natural wonders and eternal darkness.

Postojna

The Postojna basin is surrounded by rounded wooded karst hills except in the west where it is shut off by the steep Nanos plateau (1262 m). The Pivka River flows into the valley from the south and is later joined by its tributary the Nanoščica, the latter springing from numerous sources under the Nanos. At Postojna, the Pivka enters the Postojna cave, one of the most beautiful European caves that can be visited by tourists. As early as 1819 the cave had already had 104 visitors, by 1901 their

number exceeded 10.000 and until today over 25.000.000 people have visited the cave. The underground current of the Pivka River can also be followed in the Black Cave (Črna jama), which is also open to tourists, and the Pivka cave (Pivka jama) as well as the Planina cave. All those caves belong to the Postojna cave system. The Karst Research Institute in the center of Postojna houses the Karst Museum and its collection. The first hotel in Postojna opened in 1874.

In the gaping mouth of a cavern under an overhang rock on the slope of Podgorje, only 9 km from Postojna, at Predjama, is Predjama Castle of robber baron Erazem Predjamski, the subject of numerous legends. The original cave castle was first mentioned in the 13th century. In 1570 they built a new castle in front of it. Today this unique castle is an attractive tourist spot.

At the village of Zagon between Postojna and Predjama is the Betalov spodmol cave where archeological finds proved that these parts were inhabited as early as the Stone Age.

Ilirska Bistrica
Between Vremščica and the Brkini Hills the Reka River has carved a narrow winding valley with hardly any flat surface in it. The valley starts to expand at Prem, a picturesque village with stone-built houses squeezed between the Romanesque Prem castle and the local church.

Ilirska Bistrica sits in the widest part of the valley between the Brkini Hills and gently sloping wooded hillside of Snežnik (1796 m).

The Reka River springs near Zabiče close to the Croatian border. Among the Brkini Hills, near Harije, not far from the road linking Ilirska Bistrica and the Materija Valley, lie two lakes: Mola, the lower lake with a surface of 74 hectares, and Klivnik - the higher lake with a surface of 36 hectares.

A road south from Ilirska Bistrica leads via Jelšane to the nearby international border crossing with Croatia.

Central Slovenia

This is the largest Slovene region. It comprises a major part of the Ljubljana basin, a big part of the Kamnik-Savinja Alps, the Polhov Gradec Dolomites, part of the territory stretching to Notranjska and vast Kočevsko forests all the way to the state border with Croatia that runs on the Kolpa River.

Ljubljana

Over the centuries, Ljubljana's development was strongly influenced by its geographical position. The city sits in the central Slovene basin from where roads lead to the Panonian Plain, the Northern Adriatic and the East Alps.

The territory of Ljubljana has been settled for over 3000 years. During the Stone Age the Ljubljana Marshes (Ljubljansko Barje) was flooded and people settled on the shore of the lake. In the first millennium BC it was settled by the Illyrians which were followed by the Celts around 400 BC. The Romans came, built a military camp and called it Aemona. In the 5th century it was destroyed by barbaric tribes.

Ljubljana first appeared in writing as Laibach in the 12th century, and it was first mentioned as a town in the 13th century. At the beginning, it was a small, but fast-growing settlement.

The railway reached Ljubljana in 1849. In 1895 Ljubljana was destroyed by an earthquake. The first tram pulled out in 1901.

After the WW I Ljubljana became the most important city in Slovenia. It is adorned by a mighty castle atop the steep Castle Hill (Grajski hrib) with the Ljubljanica river encircling it at the foot. Two lines of buildings surround a big central market. During the last century modern town center was built on the left bank of the Ljubljanica and modern districts grew around the old and the new part: Šiška, Bežigrad, Moste, Vič and others.

The Ljubljanica gives the city a special charm. Not so long ago it was still navigable and boatmen drove

Old town core of Ljubljana (top) and the Ljubljanica embankment, in the background Šiška (taken from Ljubljana Castle).

Roofs in Stara Ljubljana (right).

Prešernov trg in the center of Ljubljana (middle right).

Dragon is the symbol of Ljubljana and is also in its coat-of-arms (bottom right).

passengers and cargo as far as Vrhnika.

The famous Slovene architect Jože Plečnik beautified Ljubljana by rebuilding and redesigning numerous parts of the city.

Ljubljana has a rich historical and cultural heritage. The city boasts a

number of museums, theaters, an opera house, a botanical garden, a zoo, etc.

Ljubljana is one of the youngest European capitals. Its position is very interesting since it is closely linked to nature. Bright city lights and green sub-alpine landscape are only few kilometers apart. All throughout the year, Ljubljana offers plenty of sports and cultural events and entertainment.

To the north of Ljubljana lies the gravely Ljubljana Plain (Ljubljansko polje). Villages along the Ljubljanica and Sava Rivers, and at the foot of the hills lie close together and have lately turned into Ljubljana suburbs. To the northeast they are Dravlje, Koseze, Šentvid, Vižmarje, Stanežiče, Brod and Tacen on the left bank of the Sava. To the north lie Brinje, Ježica and Črnuče under the hills on the left bank of the Sava, while to the east, on the wide gravely tongue between the confluence of the Sava and the Ljubljanica, lie Tomačevo, Jarše, Zadobrova, Polje, Vevče, Zalog and Kašelj To the south is Sostro.

South-east from Ljubljana, on the very edge of the Marshes run Dolenjska cesta and the railroad. Here we find settlements that still make part of the city: Galjevica and Rudnik and further on Lavrica and Škofljica where the old main road splits. One fork leads to Kočevje and the other to Novo mesto. The motorway crosses the Marshes and continues over the hills between Rudnik and Lavrica.

The Ljubljana Marshes stretch all the way from Ljubljana to Vrhnika. It is a marshy territory that has been dried up over the last centuries. The layer of peat can get down to 8 meters deep. The Marshes were filled with water until the Bronze Age. Until the 19th century settlements could only be found at the fringes of the basin and on former islands, which are now solitary hills. Ljubljansko Barje is today one of the largest grass-covered areas in Slovenia.

Golovec with its astronomic and seismologic observatories is a popular promenade.

Ig

The Ig area has typical settlements sitting under steep wooded slopes of karst plateaus. Its center is Ig around which archeologists have found several marsh dwellings. They are now exhibited in the National Museum in Ljubljana.

Iški Vintgar is a deep gorge between the Rakitna plateau and Kurešček. It has been carved out by the clear Iška stream which flows into the Ljubljanica on the Marshes.

Vrhnika

It was a river port and a military camp in the Roman times. Boating gradually disappeared after the road to Trieste had been built in 1720; people took to transport trade instead. The Idrija mercury mine also used Vrhnika as the depository.

On the slope under Sveta Trojica is the house where Ivan Cankar, considered the greatest Slovene playwright, was born. In the house there is a memorial collection.

The greatest natural sight near Vrhnika is Močilnik. The Ljubljanica resurfaces at seven different places under the karst Logatec plateau (Logaška planota).

Behind Špica (135 m) atop which is a tower with great views of the Marshes, lies the scattered village of Zaplana.

Vrhnika sits at the south-westernmost point of the Ljubljana Basin. At the edge of the Barje in the direction of Ljubljana lie villages: Stara Vrhnika, Ligojna, Drenov grič, and in the Horjul basin, among the Polhov Gradec Dolomites, Horjul. Some villages on the Marshes are built on solitary hills - Sinja Gorica, Blatna Brezovica and Bevke. Where the Marshes meet with the Logatec plateau lie Verd and Bistra with a former Carthusian monastery which today houses a technical museum with an interesting collection of old cars and many other collections. Only few kilometers further down the road lies at the mouth of the Borovnišnica valley

Polhov Gradec (top) sits among the hills which attract visitors. Sadly, this hilly country, although very close to the capital, isn't very well known among the Slovenes.

Rooms in the Polhov Gradec Castle are adorned by rich stucco work (top).

The Technical Museum at Bistra near Vrhnika is situated on the edge of the Marshes, by one of the Ljubljanica springs. A part of the museum is also the working water mill on the clear river (middle right).

The collection of old cars in Bistra is very rich (bottom right). You can see cars that belonged to Josip Broz Tito, old motorcycles, bikes and a lot of other objects. The museum is housed in a former monastery, wich is surrounded by a park.

the village of Borovnica, the starting point for the Pekel gorge. There is a path leading through the gorge which boasts a few interesting waterfalls.

Polhov Gradec

The Polhov Gradec Dolomites are like a wedge pointing towards the center of Ljubljana, stretching between the Marshes in the south and the Sava gravel pits in the north. The Šiška Hill (Šišenski hrib, 429 m) and Rožnik (394 m) are the last hills in the range. The Gradaščica valley stretches from Vič into the Dolomites. From Dobrova at the very mouth of the valley leads a parallel valley to the west. The road through it leads to Horjul..

The Gradaščica valley narrows after the village of Gabrje. After a few kilometers the winding narrow part of the valley widens into a three kilometer long and up to a kilometer wide curved basin.

Two other narrow valleys lead west from the basin, each with a road leading to the Poljanska dolina - through the left Mala voda valley to Gorenja vas, and through the right one a road with a great view via Črni vrh (861 m) and Pasje ravni (1029 m) to Poljane above Škofja Loka.

Polhov Gradec sits at the end of the picturesque Gradaščica basin at the confluence of the Mala voda and the Božna which springs under Pasja raven. The area was already settled in the Roman times. The castle in the Božna valley was built after the earthquake in 1511 had destroyed the old one. In front of the castle is a marvelous 17th century Neptune fountain. The castle also boasts a clock tower and a huge old linden tree in the castle park.

Above Polhov Gradec rises Gora (824 m) known among botanists as the area where grows Blagajev volčin *(Daphne blagayana)* which was discovered and registered as a new species in 1837 by count Blagay. The following year even the Saxon king Frederick August himself came to see the flower.

Medvode

After Medno, where the road and the railway run through a narrow part of the Sava valley between Grmada (676 m) and the Polhov Gradec Dolomites, at the confluence of the Sava and the Sora, begins the Gorenjska Plain. At the confluence sits the local center Medvode surrounded by smaller settlements. Goričane boasts a 17th century manor built by the Bishops of Ljubljana which today houses the Museum of non-European cultures.

The most interesting thing in the area is a 69 hectares big dam Zbiljsko jezero. In Dragočajna on its shore is a camp-site. The shore is unspoiled and there are hardly any buildings on it. The only settlement on the shore is Zbilje.

Smlednik, Valburga and Hraše make a clustered settlement. On the hill above Smlednik lie the ruins of a once mighty medieval Old Castle (Stari grad) and in Valburga there is a 17th century manor.

The plain between Šmarna gora and Smlednik hill is covered with forests. Numerous streams carved deep beds into the gravely ground. Behind the villages of Skaručna and Utik the plain ends with the Dobeno plateau. To the north it passes into the Kranj Plain through Repenški hrib (483 m) and Bukovniški hrib (401 m). There sits the village of Vodice.

Medvode sits in the valley at the confluence of the Sava and Sora Rivers (top).

Center of Domžale (middle right).

Krumperk Castle (bottom right) near Domžale is neglected and falling apart. Former castle work areas and the park are nowadays a horse-riding center with a famous riding school.

Domžale

The Kamniška Bistrica valley begins after Črnuče with wide gravely deposits brought by the Kamniška Bistrica River from the bosom of the Kamnik-Savinja Alps. Vast gravely deposits join the Kamniška Bistrica valley and the Kranj and Ljubljana Plains.

Domžale has developed only recently. It is the most developed town in the area. It became a market town in 1925 and it only acquired the status of a town after 1945. It has no typical town center.

Krumperk Castle used to be in the possession of the Rauber family, an old Carniolan aristocratic family that received its estates at the beginning of the 16th century. The earliest written proof of its existence dates from 1410. In 1580 the castle was rebuilt by Adam Rauber and has remained the same ever since. Today the castle houses the Equestrian Academy and nearby is the Iron Cave (Železna jama) which is opened for tourists.

Among the low rounded hills of the Zasavje Range past Dob, winds the

Moravče valley. Behind Moravče, the center of the valley, the hills pass into Limbarska gora (733 m), while in the south a hilly range with peaks up to 880 m separates the Moravče and the Sava valleys.

Mengeš

The place has been settled since prehistoric times. In the Middle Ages there was a castle perched above the town. Present castle was built in the 17th century. Menгеš received its market charter during the Habsburg rule.

The Arboretum Volčji potok is the largest arboretum in Slovenia. Behind the park is a wooded hill with the ruins of the Old Castle. The arboretum lies near Radomlje.

Villages at the foot of the Tunjice hills date from the Middle Ages. Komenda is known for its hippodrome and long tradition of pottery.

Kamnik

Kamnik is one of the oldest Slovene towns. The medieval town core is partly preserved. In the 12th century Kamnik with its castle atop the steep hill was the most influential town in Carniola. But already in the middle of the 13th century Ljubljana gained supremacy. Over the centuries Kamnik was the town of craftsmen and artisans: blacksmiths, nail-makers, leather merchants and furriers. Main sights to see are the Little Castle (Mali grad) with partly reconstructed walls, and the two-storey Romanesque church built between the 11th and 15th centuries. Some of the old town walls with a defence tower still stand near the town cemetery. Among the orchards on the slopes of the Tunjiški griči, above the old town core, sits the 16th century Renaissance manor house Zaprice. Today it houses a museum. The town also boasts a 15th century Franciscan monastery with a very interesting library. Mekinje with its 14th century monastery today also makes part of Kamnik. From the ruins of the Old Castle (Stari grad), perched atop the 180 meters high hill above the town, are great views of the upper part of the Kamniška Bistrica valley and mountains behind it, as well as of Kamnik which lies virtually at your feet.

The Nevljica stream comes from the Tuhinj Valley between the Old Castle and Mekinje and flows into the Kamniška Bistrica. The Kamniška Bistrica valley widens here and splits into two narrow gorges. From the east gorge flows the Črna stream. The villages of Črna, Potok and Krivčevo are squeezed at the bottom of the valley and higher up, on the slopes of Lom (1148 m), is Kališe. The road through this valley leads to the Upper Savinja Valley (Zgornja Savinjska dolina) over the Črnivec pass (902 m).

Kamniška Bistrica

The Kamniška Bistrica valley is in the west shut off by the Krvavec ridge and in the east by Velika planina (1666

All that is left of the former mansion house in Dol pri Ljubljani are ruins and a large castle park - a botanical garden with over 7000 plants. Sadly, it is not very well tended. Beautiful classicist pavilions have been restored (middle right). Members of the Ljubljana high society used to gather in the mansion, which was once a museum.

Geographically, Litija is the center of Slovenia. It sits by the Sava at the foot of the Zasavje Range. It is a starting point for excursions to Janče, Velika Štanga, Obolna, Sveta gora, Vače and GEOSS (Geometrical Center-Point of Slovenia) on Slivna. It is also renowned for its Mardi Gras carnival.

m), a ski center and the most authentic urbanized area in Slovenia. Old shepherds' huts have been changed into a large holiday village. Velika planina is accessible by cable car.

The Kamnik-Savinja range is the last part of the European Alps with peaks above 2000 m. The head of the Kamniška Bistrica valley is encompassed by the highest peaks of the range: Grintovec (2558 m), Skuta (2532 m), Brana (2252 m) and Planjava

Glavni trg in Kamnik (left) is only one part of the interesting old town core, above which are proudly perched partly reconstructed walls of Little Castle and the Romanesque church.

Litija

The Sava runs from Dolsko through a deep narrow valley between steep slopes. Settlements in wooded hills around the valley are small and scarce. Above Vernek stood once a castle which used to guard the transport route passing through the area.

Litija was a far nobler town in the past than it is today. Ever since the Roman times it was an important river port. It also had smelteries. In Stritarjevec (448 m) there was a lead mine which closed in 1927. Despite that Litija remained a market town until the WW II. It only became a town in the second half of this century.

Šmartno pri Litiji sits on the plain surrounding the Črni potok stream. The Črni potok valley boasts two castles, one of the same name as the stream, and another situated on the ridge of the hill between the Črni potok and the Kostrevniški potok stream. The latter is called Bogenšperk. In 1672 it was purchased by baron Janez Vajkard Valvazor, the author of the famous book *The Glory of the Duchy of Carniola*. Publishing of the book ruined him financially and he was forced to sell the castle. The castle has been renovated and today it houses a museum.

2394 m). Between the last two peaks is the saddle Kamniško sedlo (1903 m) and right behind it stretches the Logar Valley (Logarska dolina).

In a deep basin lying among white rocks and lush green vegetation springs the Kamniška Bistrica. All clear and virgin, it is immediately captured into a small lake. Then it continues its journey down the valley and soon enters the picturesque Predaselj gorge.

Vače

High up in the Zasavje hills lies to the north of Litija the village of Vače, mostly known for its Early Iron Age archaeological finds. The famous Vače situla, a bucket-like vessel from Hallstatt culture, used in rituals, was found here. Geographically, Vače is the center of Slovenia.

The Tabor camp, the 15th century fortification against Turkish invasions, is the most famous sight in the Grosuplje area. Its strong walls make it inaccessible for visitors (right).

Grosuplje

At the east of the Marshes the motorway and the railroad ascend past the village of Šmarje-Sap and descend into the Grosuplje basin. Among the undulating green hills to the east lie smaller three basins; the Višnja gora basin, the Stična basin and the Šentvid basin. The soil is very fertile and the area densely populated. Local centers have developed at the crossroads. Small basins are shut off by the low Zasavje hills in the north and by the karst plateaus in the south.

The center of this part of Central Slovenia is Grosuplje with roads leading to Novo mesto, the Krka valley, Velike Lašče and to the Zasavje. The railroad splits; one fork leads to Novo mesto and the other to Kočevje. To the north of Grosuplje is Magdalenska gora (504 m) where you can still see ruins of defense walls and archaeologists unearthed Illyrian and Celtic burial grounds.

Numerous valley streams join into the Dobravka River which disappears underground on the Radensko Plain near the ruins of Boštanj Castle. The castle was built on a solitary hill and burnt to ashes during the WW II. The Radensko Plain is a veritable miniature karst polje with swallowholes. It is the water hinterland of the Krka river.

On the karst plateau under Jelovec (666 m), near the village of Velika Lipljena lies the Mayor's cave (Županova jama) which is opened to tourists. The road past the cave comes from Ponova vas near Grosuplje and leads on to Turjak. A kilometer before the Tabor cave (Taborska jama), atop the hill sits Tabor, the best preserved defense camp from the period of Turkish invasions and a Ghotic church fortified by strong walls and defense towers.

In the Mayor's cave (small photo) near Tabor there are over 800 stairs.

Višnja Gora (middle) - once a town, today a village.

The medieval Cistercian Abbey (bottom) in Stična was first mentioned in 1136.

Višnja Gora

Višnja Gora grew under a huge castle of which only the tower still stands today. The castle has been a ruin since the 17th century. The original settlement was the Old Market (Stari trg). During the Turkish invasions the new part, fortified with walls, was built on a promontory above the basin and Višnja Gora received a town charter. Today, Višnja Gora is just a village.

Ivančna Gorica

The local center of the third basin is Ivančna gorica. Over the last years the settlement has been gradually getting a more town-like look.

In 1136 the Cistercians came to the Stična basin. They founded a monastery and the village of Stična grew around it. The Cistercians still live in the monastery. Prehistoric finds unearthed near Šentvid pri Stični testify to the early settlement of the village.

A road from Ivančna Gorica through the Višnjica valley leads to the Krka Valley. By the road lies Muljava where Josip Jurčič, the author of the first Slovene novel, was born. The church in Muljava is interesting because of the frescos dating from 1456. Ruins of two castles on the hills west of the valley are only a few hundred meters apart.

The Upper Krka Valley is one of the loveliest river valleys in Slovenia. Its wooded slopes rise gently and despite the road running along the river its shores haven't been settled. The finishing touch to the idyllic setting is added by the green colour of the clear Krka, which springs from an underground cave under Rogljevka (474 m), near the village of Gradiček.

Turjak and Velike Lašče

The Turjak Castle is one of the mightiest castles in Slovenia, situated near the road linking Škofljica and Kočevje. Its owners have made an important contribution to Slovene history. The original castle was standing already in the 10th century. It is first mentioned in writing in 1220 and its owners, the Auerspergs, in 1162. The 1511 earthquake almost completely destroyed the castle. A new one was built but it was burnt down in the WW II. Today, the castle, surrounded by vast forests, is only a poor image of ancient power.

To the south of Turjak Castle stretches a world of wooded hills with Velike Lašče as its center. Numerous small villages and settlements are scattered in the valleys. The Rašica River runs to the east and disappears as a waterfall into a sinkhole near the village of Ponikve.

Velike Lašče is a minor local center sitting at the crossroads of the road linking Ljubljana and Kočevje and roads coming from the Dobrepolje and the Bloke plateau.

Primož Trubar, who in 1550 published the first books in the Slovene, a catechism and a spelling-book, was born in the village of Rašica in 1508.

The Velike Lašče and the Dobrepolje valleys are separated by the carstified Mala gora whose slopes fall steeply into the valley. The road to the Dobrepolje leads through Ponikve. The Dobrepolje is a typical karstfield polje stretching between Mala Gora and the karst plateau Suha Krajina (Dry March). From Predstruga, the first village in the valley, the railroad runs parallel to the road.

The road and the railway to Kočevje run through a narrow valley. Atop Veliki Žrnovec (765 m), the last hill on the west side of the valley sit the ruins of a magnificent 13th century castle that used to be in the possession of the aristocratic Ortenburg family. The small river, which together with the main road and the railroad crisscrosses the valley, disappears underground near the village of Žlebič at the end of the valley.

The restored part of the former Ribnica Castle houses a museum (top).
Traditional tourist ethnological event: The Ribnica suha roba and pottery fair takes place in Ribnica every first Sunday in September. There is also a number of "intermittent" rivers flowing through the Ribnica Valley. Through Ribnica runs the Bistrica (top). All these clear streams are extremely clean.

Sodražica hides in a tributary valley (middle right). North of Sodražica rises the picturesque Slemena, a range of rounded hills.

By the Baroque church at Nova Štifta grows an enormous linden tree (bottom right) with a tree house, where the local priest likes to seek shelter from the summer heat. Nobody minds if visitors also take the opportunity.

Ribnica

Ribnica developed around the castle, surrounded by a water-filled gutter, which today houses a museum. It is the oldest parish in Dolenjska. In the past it was the center of a huge area stretching from Velike Lašče to the Kolpa River. Ribnica was granted a market charter earlier than Kočevje. The seven year Latin school was established as early as the 14th century. But Ribnica is above all known for its *suha roba* ("dry goods" - wooden household utensils) made by the locals ever since the Middle Ages.

At the beginning of the valley lies Nova Štifta with the famous 17th century Baroque church and a road leading to the Bloke plateau and Sodražica.

Another road leads northeast from Ribnica, past the France cave (Francetova jama), which is opened to tourists, to the Church of St. Ann (932 m) on the Mala Gora ridge with great views of Ribnica and the Ribnica Valley.

Kočevje

Kočevje sits in the middle of a karst polje. Its origins date to the 14th century when the Ortenburgs started to bring German settlers to work the land. At that time they built the manor house in Mahovnik and a settlement developed around it later on. In 1847 coal was discovered at Šalka vas near Kočevje. The lake Rudniško jezero between Kočevje and Šalka vas sits on the former coal mine and is a kilometer long and up to 60 meters deep. Since an underground stream constantly brings in fresh water, the lake is crystal clear. Over the last years its shore has been cleaned as well, which makes it increasingly visited by tourists.

Through the Kočevje Plain winds the small Rinža River which disappears into the sinkholes immediately after Kočevje.

Behind Mala Gora stretch vast forests of the Kočevski Rog. The Kočevsko Plain is surrounded by forests stretching all the way to the Krka and Kolpa Rivers and further on to the Croatian Gorski Kotar, and on the other side to Snežnik and further on to Ilirska Bistrica. Forests abound in game, you can even chance upon a bear, wolf or lynx.

The German-speaking Kočevars left the country at the beginning of the WW II and forests have overgrown over 50 abandoned villages. In the WW II the Kočevski Rog sheltered the headquarters of the Slovene resistance - it was called Baza 20.

One of the roads from Kočevje leads through Dolga vas and Livold where a side road branches off to the southeast and leads to Bela Krajina, while the main road turns south towards a number of small settlements in the Kolpa valley and brings us via the Brod na Kolpi border crossing to the Croatian Gorski Kotar.

The whole area to the south east, between Kočevje and the Croatian border, was a closed territory after the WW II. Kočevska Reka in the Goteniška dolina valley was its center.

In the formerly closed district under Kočevska reka is a 2km long dam (top). "Former" Slovene politicians came to the district for fun, hunting and fishing and the latter is also the reason why they built the dam on the Mokri potok stream. Today the district is open and the dam abounds in carp.

The steep stony Loška stena (875 m) rises above the valley of the bordering Kolpa River.

On a rocky cliff above the Kolpa valley is Kostel Castle (bottom right). During the Turkish invasions the well fortified castle played an important defense role and provided shelter for local inhabitants. Today the castle is under reconstruction. It might become a popular tourist spot in the future.

Dam on the local stream in a wild gorge under Kočevska Reka is 2 km long while the surrounding forests are full of game. Areas so unspoiled and so unsettled are scarce in Europe.

State border with Croatia runs along the deep Čabranka valley until it joins the Kolpa River and then along the beautiful Kolpa valley.

On a gravely promontory above the confluence of the two rivers sits a touristically developing village of Osilnica and on the slopes of Goteniška Gora lies a number of smaller settlements.

Further down the Kolpa lies the valley Poljanska dolina one of the remotest areas in Slovenia with Stari Trg ob Kolpi as its center. In Predgrad is an old castle building and in the deep Kolpa valley some smaller settlements. The Poljanska dolina was named after the Ortenburg Castle which was built there in the 14th century. Today it is an area which offers a lot of farmhouse accommodation and the Kolpa River gives it a special magic.

Dolenjska

Dolenjska is like the softness of an enchanted song and such are its people, too. Its low hills scattered with castles, country crisscrossed by green rivers, streams and forests, and facetiousness and hospitality of the locals can be met at every step.

Magic birch groves of Bela Krajina sing a different tune. They leave behind a tale reminiscent of our childhood. Rich folk tradition, typical songs, noble wine and genuine food are relaxing for the eyes as well as the soul.

Novo mesto

Rudolfswert was founded in 1365 by a Habsburg, Rudolf II, who named it after himself. It was named Novo mesto in the 15th century.

The town was built on a high promontory above the Krka River Houses in the old town core line the right-angled town square. The town was fortified by strong city walls and a number of defense towers. But the best protection was the Krka River. Although often under siege in times of Turkish invasions, the town was never taken. In those days the town was in its prime.

Franciscan monks came to town in 1492 and in 1746 they established a gymnasium. Of great importance is also the Dolenjska Museum whose collections are exhibited in the old building of Križantija.

Today, Novo mesto, extending on both banks of the Krka, is the industrial and cultural center of Dolenjska. On the plain between Novo mesto and Straža is an aircraft center and to the north and west stretch green hills with tilled valleys and slopes. The whole area is densely populated.

Between the villages of Brusnice and Šentjernej lies the Gracarjev turn Castle which was only given today's structure in the 16th century. Only a kilometer to the south is the Vrhovo Castle, and a bit further south, above the village of Cerovo at the foot of the Gorjanci, is

Collections in the Dolenjski Muzej in Novo mesto testify to the rich history of the area (top right).

From Marof, popular Novo mesto promenade, extends a great view of the town center (top). Another popular excursion spot is Trška gora, a renowned wine-growing district. Green banks of the Krka also invite us for long dreamy walks.

The Capitol Church of St. Nicholas (middle right) is the oldest architectural monument in Novo mesto and one of the finest Gothic churches in Slovenia.

Gracarjev turn (bottom right) is just one of the numerous castles in the Krka valley - the valley of castles.

the small Prežek Castle which was first mentioned in writing in 1180.

The best known castle in Dolenjska is Otočec situated on a tiny island in

the middle of the Krka river. The castle is a rare example of a water castle in Slovenia. Its history begins far back in the Middle Ages. During the WW II it was severely damaged, but it has been rebuilt and turned into a hotel.

State border with Croatia runs on the ridges of the Gorjanci via the highest peak Trdinov vrh (1178 m). Above the village of Gabrje is Gospodična (828 m) with great views of the area.

There are two other castles nearby: Hmeljnik near the village Karteljevo and Stari grad nad Otočcem. Hmeljnik sits on the ridge of Hmeljniški boršt and can easily be spotted from the main road linking Ljubljana and Zagreb. It was first mentioned in writing in 1217 and it is one of the most important Romanesque castles in Slovenia. Sadly the castle suffered a similar fate than so many other castles in Slovenia. It was burnt down in 1942 and after the war even shelled and mined.

The Old Castle (Stari grad) sits on the slope of Trška gora, surrounded by vineyards and many wine cellars. This castle can also be easily spotted from the main road. The first Stari grad knight was Albert who lived in the first half of the 13th century. The castle has been restored, for which we can thank Krka, the Novo mesto pharmaceutical company.

Only a few kilometers from Otočec is the spa Šmarješke Toplice. Tourism has its origins in 1790 but they were only modernized in the period between the two world wars.

Dolenjske Toplice

In the middle of the wide Krka Valley above Novo mesto sits Meniška vas and behind the hill lies Dolenjske Toplice, the oldest thermal spa in Dolenjska.

Through the Črmošnjica valley leads a road to Bela Krajina, and up the slope of Rog another one to the WW II museum - the Baza 20 complex.

Šentjernej

Near Šentjernej, in a secluded valley under the Gorjanci, lies the Carthusian monastery Pleterje. It was founded in 1407 by the Counts of Cilli. In 1899 it was bought by the Carthusians and rebuilt. The only building left from the original monastery is the Ghotic church. The Carthusians have in possession around 20 hectares of walled grounds with buildings on 4 hectares.

Trebnje

The ribbon settlement is situated the green hilly land by the "intermittent" Temenica and is the center of this part of Dolenjska. The Temenica disappears in the swallowholes near Ponikve, and when its flow is bigger, also in the Risavica swallowhole. In prehistoric times the town was settled by the Celts and later on Romans have built here a military camp Praetorium Latobicorum. Today there is a well-known gallery of self-made painters in Trebnje.

The Mirna Valley

At the beginning of the Mirna Valley is Mirna. Ruins of the Mirna Castle (Mirenski grad) perched above a tributary valley are slowly being rebuilt. Settlements are scattered on the edges of the valley only. Numerous castles at the side of the valley testify to former importance of Mirna. On Debenec (547 m) is a tower which has great views of the valley.

In the last, wide part of the valley, sits Mokronog which was already inhabited by the Celts. The whole area of Mokronog is hilly and forested. Tiny narrow valleys and brooks meander among the hills. The area is scattered

White-hooded monks spend their days in the solitude of their rooms or in one of the rich libraries of the Carthusian monastery in Pleterje (top right).

All the monastery buildings are covered with black slate (top). The history of the monastery is similar to that of the Stična abbey. It was founded in the Middle Ages when it also reached its prime. It was later abolished, but the monks returned in the 19th century. Today there are only some 20 monks living in it.

The Krka Valley downstream from Žužemberk (top right).

A particularity in the upper part of the Krka are small tuff waterfalls which offer great fun to bathers and kayak paddlers (center right).

Škrljevo Castle in the Mirna Valley (bottom right).

with small settlements, some of which make small villages but there is also a number of isolated farms. People are friendly and hospitable and the nature charming.

Žužemberk

The Krka is the only Slovene river with small waterfalls which are the consequence of the water flowing over tuff mounds. In this part the Krka Valley cuts the karst plateau Suha Krajina in half. The northern half lies between the valley of Krka and Trebnje. The largest settlement in this part is Dobrnič. The southern part lies between Mala Gora and the Kočevski Rog. Roads from Žužemberk, Dvor and Fužine lead to this part of Suha Krajina. Villages on the plateau are small and poor.

Žužemberk is situated on both banks of the Krka. On the edge of the terrace above the Krka lie the ruins of the Žužemberk castle which are lately being rebuilt. The castle was burnt down in the WW II and so was the parish church. A few years ago a new parish church was built. The castle was first mentioned in writing in 1295 when it was bought by Albert II, a Count of Gorizia. From 1469 to the WW II it was in the possession of the Auerspergs, Counts of Turjak.

Dvor had the first Slovene machine shop that also produced arms, which they delivered even to the Serbs for the first armed rebellion against the Turks. After the construction of the southern railway the shop, owned by the counts of Turjak, went bankrupt.

In the village of Soteska, on the bank of the Krka, lie ruins of a castle which was in the possession of the Counts of Cilli.

Bela Krajina (White Carniola)

It is an undulating plain surrounded by the Kočevski Rog in the west, the Gorjanci in the north, and the Kolpa River in the south and east. The whole plain is eroded, full of sinkholes and covered with heavy red karst soil. Bela Krajina is at its most beautiful in spring.

At the foot of Poljanska gora springs out the Lahinja river and its numerous tributaries. The small river meanders among low hills of Bela Krajina and soon flows into the Kolpa which then makes a big curve around the Metlika Plain and leaves Slovenia at the village of Rakovec. The state border with Croatia and the Kolpa River go their separate ways from here on.

Panonian climate allows the inhabitants of Bela Krajina to grow vine. Winters are mild and summers hot with little precipice. For centuries, the region has been one of the poorest in Slovenia which consequently led to huge emigration at the turn of the century. It was only after the WW II that its economy recovered. During the WW II, Bela Krajina was the center of Slovene resistance.

Its villages have preserved the most of traditional folklore in Slovenia. The area is named after traditional white clothes worn by men and women in their everyday life up to the WW II. Today, the costumes are only worn at traditional dance festivals.

Metlika

Metlika was first mentioned in writing in the 13th century. It was given a charter in 1335. Its position by the Kolpa River made it an important military camp and market center. The Metlika Castle houses the Bela Krajina Museum. In Rosalnice, not far from town are three churches built in a row that used to be the seat of the first Metlika parish.

Gradac in Bela Krajina sits by the Lahinja River at the road linking Metlika and Črnomelj. The village is built around the 13th century castle.

The Semič wine-growing district is very famous (top). Hospitality of the locals, unspoiled nature, bathing, boating, fishing, varied traditional food and, of course, the wine, bring more and more people to Bela Krajina.

Tri fare (to right) by the village of Rosalnice near Metlika has been there for centuries. Its name is not derived from three parishes which might have had their seat there, but from three churches which share only one belfry, and which are, God knows why, squeezed together behind one wall.

Metlika Castle houses the Bela Krajina and Firefighting Museums (middle right).

Strong current of the Krupa River comes from the karst underground under a steep rocky wall (bottom right). In the Postojna cave lives a veritable cave dragon - the "human fish" whose skin colour resembles that of a human. In the caves of Bela Krajina, also by the source of the Krupa, live black "human fish".

Črnomelj

Črnomelj sits on a promontory at the confluence of the Lahinja and Dobličica rivers. It was a market town already in the 13th century and was given a charter in the 15th century. During the Turkish invasions a strong wall was built around it.

At Rožanec, near the railroad between Črnomelj and Sremič is a Mithraic shrine. On Kučer (222 m) near the village of Podzemelj, archaeologists have unearthed the richest site in Bela Krajina. Copper and iron objects testify to the importance of the settlement in the prehistoric times.

Semič

Semič sits at the foot of the last Gorjanci hills. Steep slope looks like a colourful patchwork of vineyards and wine cellars. Atop Sv. Lovrenc (546 m) are ruins of the Smuk Castle and at Stranska vas near Semič lies, under a rocky cliff, the spring of the Krupa River. There is a road leading from Semič through the Črmošnjica valley to Dolenjske Toplice and Novo mesto.

Posavje (The Sava basin)

Sevnica

Where the Sava valley widens lies Sevnica, and a bit further south is Boštanj. The Sava is joined by the Sevnična stream from the north and the Mirna River flowing from among the Dolenjsko hills from the south. The entrance into the Mirna Valley used to be protected by the Tariški grad Castle and the narrow part of the Sava valley by the Boštanj Castle.

The picturesque old town core is squeezed between Castle Hill and the Sava. The Sevnica Castle is first mentioned in writing in 1309 but it had been built far earlier. Its present form dates from the 16th century. Near the castle is also Lutrovska klet with reach pre-Baroque figural paintings. It was used for religious purposes and as a Protestant shelter. Jurij Dalmatin, who was the first to translate the Bible into the Slovene, also used to teach in it. Today it houses cultural events.

Between 1970 and 1978, archaeologists unearthed Ajdovski gradec (436 m) above the village of Vranje near Sevnica. Ajdovski Gradec used to be one of the largest Early Christian centers in the Alps and the Danube basin. The size of the church - it was a basilica - was 14 x 7 m. Several other buildings were unearthed. The whole complex was burnt down at the end of the 6th century.

From Breg pri Kompolju leads a road to Lisca (948 m) which has great views of the surroundings.

Brestanica

At Brezovo, not far from Sevnica, the Sava turns east and runs across a kilometer wide plain - the Pijavško polje. The Brestanica stream flows into the Sava at Brestanica. In the Middle Ages the entrance into the valley was protected by the Brestanica Castle, first mentioned in writing already in 895. Brestanica, the market town which developed under the castle, used to be called Rajhenburg.

Capuchin library in the center of Krško (right) is one of the numerous witnesses of the rich history of these parts. Others are archeological finds from the Stone, Bronze and Iron Ages, remains of the Roman town Neviodunum, early Christian center on Ajdovski gradec above Vranje, Brestanica Castle (middle right) and numerous other castles in this fertile wine-growing area which is as small and varied as Slovenia.

Leskovec is now a Krško suburb (bottom right).

An old legend has it that there were two brothers in the 15th century that lived in a castle. They had a fight and one of them built a new castle by the Sava. The Rajhenburg Castle was bought by the French monks Trappists in 1881 and changed into a monastery. Trappists lived in it until the WW II. During the WW II it was a detention camp through which over 45 000 Slovenes have passed when the Germans exiled or deported them to concentration camps. The castle today houses the museum whose collections remind us of those difficult times.

Sevnica Castle (top) is perched above the old town core of Sevnica (left). It houses the School and Firefighting Museums.

Krško

Krško sits at the beginning of the Posavje Plain between the Sava and Libna gora (354 m). The old town core lies on the other side of the river, squeezed between the river and the slopes of Trška gora (369 m).

In Roman times the road from *Neviodunum* to *Celeia* led through Krško. During the Middle Ages a strongly fortified castle guarded the passage from the plain to the Sava valley. The town was fortified by walls as well and there was a river port on the Sava.

The first school in Krško was established as early as 1564 by Adam Bohorič who wrote the first Slovene grammar book. The system of writing he used was named after him "bohoričica" and remained in use up to 1839.

Above Leskovec, a Krško suburb, is the Šrajbarski turn Castle. In its neighbourhood the enlisted army strongly defeated a horde of peasants during peasant uprisings.

The road from Krško joins the main road from Ljubljana to Zagreb at the Krakovski gozd forest known for its centennial oak trees. It is the largest flatland forest in Slovenia.

Near Krško is also the nuclear power station, the only one in Slovenia.

Along the road linking Ljubljana and Zagreb, near the village Drnovo, was a Roman town Neviodunum.

Brežice

Brežice lies at the confluence of the Sava and Krka Rivers. It used to be an important fortification protecting the passage from Panonia to the sub-Alpine regions. In the 13th century it had a mint and coined money. In 1515 the castle was taken by the rebelling peasants. At the next uprising in 1573 the peasants suffered a crushing defeat. Their leader Matija Gubec was thrown in jail in the Mokrice Castle. Today the Brežice Castle houses rich collections of the Posavje Museum.

Mokrice Castle sits atop a hill above the Koričanski potok. It is surrounded by a 200 year old English park with a surface of 60 hectares. It was first mentioned in writing in 1444 when it was in the possession of German feudal families. The castle as it stands today was built in the 16th century. In 1944 it was attacked by the partisans but because of its strong defence it wasn't taken. The Mokrice Castle is thus one of the few castles in this part of Slovenia that survived the WW II. Now it is a hotel with a golf course in the park.

The Čateške Toplice spa is only a few kilometers away from Brežice. Water temperature of thermal springs exceeds 50°C.

Above the old town core of Brežice reigns a water tower (top left). The Brežice castle boasts the largest Festive hall with Baroque paintings in Slovenia.

The former monastery by Kostanjevica na Krki houses the Božidar Jakac Gallery and in the park is a Forma Viva (top left).

Mokrice Castle can easily be spotted from the main road linking Ljubljana and Zagreb. The castle, now a prestigious hotel, is surrounded by a large English park with a golf course.

The wine road through the Bizeljsko-Sremiš wine district is accompanied by the noise of klopotci in Pišece (middle right). It is lined by a number of private wine cellars where home made food is served with top quality wines.

The work areas of the Orešje Castle (bottom right) in Bizeljsko region house huge wine cellars. The castle sits atop a hill, just like the Pišece castle which is sadly falling apart. The Brežice Castle, on the other hand, was completely restored and houses rich collections of the Posavje Museum. Unfortunately, the Museum is only opened on week days, in the afternoons.

Kostanjevica na Krki

From Otočec the Krka wriggles like a snake across the vast flat plain. In its sharpest loop at the foot of Gorjanci lies Kostanjevica na Krki surrounded by water from all sides. Kostanjevica na Krki is one of the oldest Slovene towns. It was granted a town charter at the beginning of the 13th century. Today it is the smallest Slovene town. The monastery near the town was built in 1234 and it used to rule over 100 villages in the Middle Ages. It is situated near the village of Orehovec, under the steep slope of Veliki Trebež (823 m) in the Gorjanci. It was dissolved by the edict issued by Emperor Joseph II. Today the monastery building houses a gallery and a Forma Viva.

Not far away is the Kostanjevica cave (Kostanjeviška jama), open to tourists.

Bizeljsko

The Bizeljsko hills are scattered with numerous vineyards and isolated farms. In the remote valley under Velika Vagla, atop a rocky hill is sadly falling apart Pišece Castle. It was first mentioned in writing in 1329 and was built as it stands today in 1867.

At the village of Orešje is Bizeljsko Castle with forest-covered slopes of Kunšperk (597 m) rising above it. Today the castle is part of the Trebče Memorial Park.

Zasavje (The Sava Valley)

Zagorje

Several narrow valleys cut into the Zasavje Hills. The first is the valley of the Medija River. In the wider part of the valley, behind the gorge between Vrh (679 m) and Iskranjca (672 m), lies Zagorje, the oldest coal-mining town in Slovenia. Coal has been mined here since 1755.

There are two other settlements that make part of Zagorje - Dolenja vas and Kisovec.

Near Izlake is the spa Medijske Toplice and by the road to Moravče is the Medija Manor which used to belong to the Valvasor family. Atop a steep hill above the Kotedrščica brook valley lie the ruins of a once mighty Gamberk Castle. The castle was built at the end of the 12th century.

Trbovlje

Trbovlje is the center of the so called "black district" - the coal-mining district, and of Zasavje. It is the largest coal-mining center in Slovenia. Coal was discovered in 1805 and later on the glass factory was built. The town sits in the narrow Trboveljščica valley.

Hrastnik

The Hrastnik basin is separated from Trbovlje only by a ridge-like threshold. Hrastnik has also developed by the coal mines.

Wooded hills separate those parts from the Savinja valley which can be reached by an interesting serpentine mountain road leading from Trbovlje to Prebold. Peaks higher than 1000 meters are scarce among those hills.

Zidani most

The Sava valley remains very narrow from Hrastnik to Radeče. At Zidani most, a few kilometers before Radeče, the Savinja from the north flows into the Sava. Zidani most is also an important crossroads. Although the railway station is known beyond our borders, Zidani most remains no more than a middle-sized village.

In Zasavje, the Sava runs trough a narrow valley (bottom). Under steep slopes, rising high above the rivers bed, there,s hardly enough space for the road and the railroad. Villages and towns are in the tiny side valleys. The only exception is Radeče.

Zagorje (top) owes his developpment mostly to coal-mining and industry.

Radeče (left) sitsat the confluence of the Sopota and Sava Rivers. Higher above the Sopota valley are steep hills. The small village of Svibno (bottom) left) sitson one of them.

Radeče

Njivice near Radeče was already settled in the Early Stone Age. Radeče was granted a town charter in 1925.

The Sopota valley cuts far west under Kum (1220 m) which is also called the Triglav of Zasavje. The Sopota valley is surrounded by cone-like peaks. On one of them sits Svibno, a small village, which was a market town already in the Middle Ages. In the 10th century a castle was built atop the cone peak above the village. The Sopota valley is settled with few smaller settlements and numerous isolated farms. A larger village in the valley is Podkum.

Koroška

The Koroška forests are a veritable paradise for anyone who appreciates peace and quiet. Holidaying in Koroška offers tranquillity and quenches curiosity the city man constantly seeks and needs. There are countless trails leading from peak to peak. Experiences are so fulfilling that their memories stay alive for a long time.

There is nothing like living in one of the green Koroška valleys for a while. Be it the Mežica, the Mislinja or the Drava valley, they all make you feel as if time stopped for a brief moment. And its history proves that Koroška is a very old country.

Slovenj Gradec

For centuries, the town has been the center of the valley. Under Grajski grič (526 m) the Romans built a settlement Colatio and an important road passed through it as well. Atop Grajski grič they built a temple. The castle built on Grajski grič in the 9th century was turned into a church in the 11th and the tower was used as a belfry. As a market town, Slovenj Gradec is first mentioned in writing in 1251 and only a few years later it was granted a town charter.

The Mislinja Valley

The Mislinja River comes through a narrow gorge, Mislinjski graben, right from the heart of the Pohorje Massif. In the first wider part of the valley sits the picturesque village of Mislinja. The river flows from here through a wide, mostly flat plain where we find the villages of Šentilj pod Turjakom, Dovže, Mislinjska Dobrava, Turiška vas and Šmartno. Through a parallel tributary valley under last fringes of the Kamnik-Savinja Alps flows into the Mislinja the Jenina stream. At the entrance to the tributary valley sits Stari trg.

Round church of St. John the Baptist in Spodnja Muta (top left). Its name tells us that it is very old. In 1052 it was consecrated by the pope Leon IX who travelled through Carinthia.

The green Mislinja valley just asks us to stop, take a rest and enjoy the beauty of the idyllic landscape.

The lead mine in Črna na Koroškem is now closed, but it has been turned into a museum (right).

The Meža Valley

Under Olševa (1929 m) and Peca (2126 m) springs the Meža River. The state border with Austria runs on mountain ridges from Olševa, over Moraldčev vrh (1490 m), Snežnik (1544 m) and Mozganov vrh (1575 m) to Peca and then further north along the lower ridges.

The Meža cuts a narrow valley to the south. At Črna na Koroškem, the Meža is joined by two other streams: the Bistra, which springs under Raduha (2062 m), and the Javorski potok, which springs out in the opposite wooded range. In all three valleys isolated farms are scattered among torrential ravines.

Črna na Koroškem is an old mining settlement. Furnaces have been built here as early as the 17th century.

Further down the valley is Žerjav

which also boasts quite some mining equipment.

Where the Meža leaves the gorge lies Mežica. Up to few decades ago the area lived exclusively off mining but now it is fast turning to tourism. The Mežica mercury and zinc mine is now opened to tourists.

From Mežica the Meža flows through a nice valley lying among wooded hills with a number of isolated farms. The road and railroad from the Podjuna valley in Austria lead via the mountain pass at Holmec along the Meža via Prevalje and Ravne na Koroškem to Dravograd.

Dravograd

Dravograd sits at the confluence of the Drava nad Muta Rivers. Old Dravograd was built around a 12th century castle on a high terrace above the Drava, which makes a loop right under the town. It was in that time that the town received its market charter.

A road from Dravograd leads via the village of Vič to the border crossing with Austria which is only 3 km away. From Dravograd, the Drava meanders through a narrow valley. All the way to Maribor the main road runs along the left bank and the railway along the right bank of the river.

At the beginning of the valley is the Pukštanj castle. The valley widens at the village of Trbonje. On wide terraces on the north bank lie Muta and Radlje ob Dravi which were, together with Vuzenica, granted market charters already in the Middle Ages. On the hill above Radlje lie ruins of the Old Castle (Stari grad) and there was also a Dominican monastery in the market town.

The Mučka Bistrica stream flows from Austria. It cuts a narrow valley through the Kobansko hills and flows into the Drava at Muta. On the south bank of the Drava, at the confluence of the Drava and the Crkvenica stream, is Vuzenica.

Drava is dammed several times in this part. Hydro power stations are built at Dravograd, above Vuzenica and in the narrow under Vuhred.

Štajerska (Styria)

Štajerska is a land of friendly people, noblest wines and excellent traditional dishes. Numerous thermal springs attract travelers. It abounds in cultural monuments and merry events. Extremely rich cultural and historical heritage can be enjoyed at every step. Numerous castles, manor houses, monasteries and famous churches greet visitors at every corner.

Štajerska is also a land of high mountains and beautiful valleys. Is there anyone who hasn't yet heard of the valleys Logarska dolina or Robanov kot? Of Styrian lakes and fishponds, of the hilly Haloze, Slovenske Gorice or Kozjansko?

Štajerska is interesting in every season from every aspect, be it its winter sports resorts, summer adventures or autumn grape harvests. May your path lead to this green land, too!

Savinjska (The Savinja region)

Celje

Celje developed on the plain at the entrance to the narrow valley the Savinja River makes on its way to the Sava. It has always been a crossroads of routes coming from all directions. The original Illyrian settlement Celeia was there 3500 years ago. It was called Claudia Celeia under the Romans and was one of the biggest Roman towns on Slovene territory. Rich archaeological finds testify to the Roman wealth. The town was destroyed during the great migrations. It was mentioned again in 1125. In the 14th and 15th centuries the town was ruled by the Counts of Cilli and it thrived. The Counts of Cilli ruled from the castle built on Grajski hrib (407 m) above the city. The castle used to protect the entrance to the narrow Savinja Valley. In the second half of the 15th century the Counts of Cilli died out and their possessions were inherited by the Habsburgs.

The third largest Slovene town is Celje (top). Old town core preserved the structure of a medieval town.

Only 10 km south of Celje in the Savinja Valley, sits Laško (middle). Hot thermal springs were known already by the Romans. And every visitor to Slovenia knows the Zlatorog beer, brewed in Laško since 1825.

The Old Castle above Laško has been completely restored and today cultural and tourist events take place there.

The railway came to town in 1846 and brought about the beginning of industrialization. That led to fast urbanization of neighbouring villages and they consequently united with the city. At present Celje is the third largest Slovene town.

The 16th century feudal manor Stara grofija houses the Celje Museum. The Church of St. Mary was a part of a former Minorite monastery from the 13th century and the Counts of Cilli are buried in it

Laško

Between Celje and its confluence with the Sava, the Savinja runs through a narrow valley which cuts deep into the Posavje hills. The area is very mountain-like. The first village from Zidani most up the valley is Obrežje. A bit further up, at the village of Gračnica, the Savinja is joined by the Gračnica stream which comes from a long meandering tributary valley through which leads a road via Jurklošter and Planina pri Sevnici, under Bohor (1023 m) to Kozjansko. There is a 12th century Carthusian monastery in Jurklošter.

The Savinja Valley slightly widens north of Gračnica. Among dark forests, in the middle of a park full of exotic plants, sits the spa Rimske Toplice.

Thermal springs can also be found only a few kilometers up the valley, near Laško which is the largest settlement in the valley. Laško was granted a market charter in 1227 but it did not acquire the status of a town until 1927. The Baroque castle from 1675 houses a museum. The parish church in Laško also has a rich history, it dates from the Romanesque and Ghotic periods. The church as it stands today was built in the Baroque period. On the steep slope between the Savinja and Hum (538 m) sits the rebuilt Old Castle (Stari grad).

Thermal spa in Laško has been known since the second half of the 19th century. Among the Slovenes Laško is best known for its brewery which has been brewing beer since 1825.

Šentjur

Among the first Kozjansko Hills lies the lake Slivniško jezero which is also called the Kozjansko sea. The lake is actually a dam on the Voglajna River, with a depth of 14 m and a surface of 86 hectares. After the dam, the Voglajna flows along the foot of Gradišče (441 m) and then through the valley between Gradišče and Prednja gora (454 m). The meandering river almost completely encircles Prednja gora then turns around Rifnik to the Šentjur plain and finally to Štore and Celje. On a shelf on the slope of Rifnik (568 m) are the ruins of a Krško Castle that later came into the possession of the Counts of Cilli. There was an important settlement on top of Rifnik already in the Antiquity. Excellent views are also from Resevnik (630 m), Rifnik's western neighbour.

Šentjur pri Celju is a local center with a road and rail line leading from Celje to Rogatec.

Rogatec and Podčetrtek

Rogatec was a parish as early as the Middle Ages but it was not granted a market charter until 1875.

In the tributary valley under Boč (979 m) is Lemberg which acquired the status of a market town in 1244 but today it is just a small village and there is no trace of its former economic power. Only a few kilometers away, under Zbelovska Gora, lies the village Sladka gora with its famous pilgrimage church.

Thermal springs of Rogaška Slatina were first mentioned in the 11th century and mineral water has been sold since the 17th century. Well tended gardens are lined with spa buildings and surrounded by wooded hills.

Between Šmarje pri Jelšah and the Sotla valley stretches a hilly world with a number of isolated farms, mostly scattered on the ridges. Streams flow into the lake Slivniško jezero and into the Sotla. In the Tinjski potok valley, under Žusem (596 m) which has great views, is Loka pri Žusmu. On Žusem

From the central courtyard of the Podsreda Castle (top left) lead entrances to the museum and gallery rooms and to the reconstructed castle kitchen. Especially interesting is the castle jail, hidden under the stairs.

At Olimje near Podčetrtek is a Renaissance castle with round towers (bottom right). In the 1550 castle there was a Pauline monastery with its own pharmacy in the 17th and 18th centuries. The pharmacy has been completely restored and the

is a church with two belfries, and on the ridge under the peak ruins of a castle.

There is another castle perched above Podčetrtek which used to protect the route to the Sotla valley. Nearby is the thermal spa Atomske Toplice. In Olimje near Podčetrtek are the remains of the Minorite monastery with defence towers and an old pharmacy.

monks will kindly take you to see it. There is another Podsreda Castle (Podsreški grad) only 5 km from Podsreda on the north slope of Orlica (686 m). The castle was built in the first half of the 12th century and despite later changes it managed to preserve its original core almost unchanged. When it was build it was one of the five major feuds of Krško and the seat of the land court. It has been systematically restored since 1983.

Kozjansko

The Zasavje Hills end with the Kozjansko Hills. In the southeast, Kozjansko borders the mountainous slope of Bohor (1023 m), in the east the Sotla valley through which runs the state border with Croatia, and in the north, it borders Rudnica (626 m).

Kozje, the center of Kozjansko sits in the wider part of the Bistrica valley. There are other villages in the valley as well: Lesično, Zagorje and Planina pri Sevnici. A road to Sevnica runs through these parts. At the foot of Orlica, near Podsreda, the Bistrica brook turns east to the Sotla. Above Podsreda we can still see a Romanesque castle which still looks as it did in the 12th century.

A road from Podsreda leads west via Senovo to Krško, and another one east along the Bistrica to the Sotla valley. In the middle of a wide plain lies Bistrica ob Sotli.

The road and the rail line lead up the Sotla via Imena to Podčetrtek and down the Sotla to Bizeljsko and further on to Brežice. Here, the state border with Croatia runs on the Sotla.

The Lower Savinja Valley

In 1760 the Novo Celje Castle was built near Petrovče and the Vienna Schonbrun was used as the model. Dobriša vas and Vrbje are also nearby.

Before it reaches Prebold and Latkova vas, the Savinja turns northwest. The largest towns in this part of the valley are Šempeter and Žalec, the latter is also known as the hop growing center. Hops from Žalec are sold all over the world. It is interesting that Žalec received the market charter before Celje and yet Celje developed much faster than Žalec.

The village of Podlog near Šempeter is a starting point for the Pekel cave (Jama Pekel) which is open to tourists and where springs the Peklenščica stream. The cave has two entrances linked by a forest study path.

Vransko development was paramount to the development of traffic. In the 16th century it was a mail stop between Ljubljana and Graz. It became a market town in 1868.

At Dobrteša vas near Šempeter the road splits. One road and a rail line run along the east bank of the Savinja leading to the Paka valley. There is another road from Polzela leading via hilly Andraž and the Kavče village to the Šalek Valley (Šaleška dolina). Another road and railway leading to the Šalek Valley run more to the west through the Paka valley. The Paka flows into the Savinja at a mountain. A bit further up, at the beginning of the valley is Šmartno ob Paki.

There is yet another road leading to this parts from the main road linking Ljubljana and Maribor from Šentrupert. On its right side near the villages of Gomilsko and Šmatevž is Lake Žovnek (Žovneško jezero) with the ruins of the Žovnek Castle perched above it. It was this castle that the family of the Counts of Cilli originated from.

Near the Braslovče village is Lake Braslovče (Braslovško jezero). Right after Letuš the valley narrows and the road splits. One fork leads east to Šmartno ob Paki and the other one north-west through a few kilometers of a narrow valley to the Upper Savinja Valley.

The Roman Necropolis in the center of Šempeter has long been a reminder of the ancient history of the town (top). In 166, the Savinja flooded and destroyed the settlement and high tombs made of Vitanje marble. In 1952 the necropolis was unearthed, restored and turned into apark.

Most of the tilling lands in the Lower Savinja Valley are covered with hops (middle right). Hop-vines are grown on hop poles or ropes and their cone-like fruits are used for brewing beer. Hop cones add bitter flavour to the beer, but they also contain a nice smelling oil. In Slovenia, hops are grown in this valley only.

Old industrial town sits on the south edge of the Lower Savinja valley, above the right bank of the Bolska River. By the town lies the Renaissance Prebold Mansion built in the 16th century. Tourism is taking off here. In Prebold there are two camping sites and the surroundings abound in natural, cultural and historical sights which attract visitors.

Upper Savinja Valley

The valley begins with the small Mozirje basin. The largest settlement in the Upper Savinja Valley is Mozirje which was settled already by the Romans. In Mozirje lies Savinjski gaj, a famous botanical garden and above Mozirje rises Golte, a winter resort. To Golte leads the longest cable car in Slovenia.

During the Middle Ages the Vrbovec castle in Nazarje, which has been restored, protected the narrow passage between Mozirje and Nazarje. On the terrace above the castle sits a Franciscan monastery whose church has two belfries.

From the tributary Zadrečka Valley, flows the Dreta brook. The road through the valley brings us to the Gornji Grad basin surrounded by wooded plateaus Dobrovlje and Menina, and by the Veliki Rogatec range (1557 m). The center of the basin is Gornji Grad where the Benedictines built a monastery in 1140. In the 15th century the monastery was dissolved and the estates presented to the Bishops of Ljubljana. It was the center of the Ljubljana diocese until 1783 the baroque Cathedral was built under their rule. Under their rule the Baroque cathedral was built. Gornji Grad was granted a market charter in the 14th century and acquired the status of a town in 1928.

In the wide deposited part of the Upper Savinja Valley, north of Nazarje, lie two other interesting settlements - Rečica and Ljubno which were both granted a market charter as early as the 15th century. Ljubno used to be an important timber trade center. Raftsmen used to raft their lumber rafts all the way to the Sava and sometimes even to Belgrade. The rafting trade stopped in 1954. At Ljubno pri Savinji, the Savinja

The Vrbovec Castle (top left) in Nazarje has been almost completely restored. Today, the community administration and several companies have their seat in it. How inappropriate for a castle ...

On the hill above the Vrbovec castle is a monastery in whose library you can find a number of old manuscripts and the 1584 original Jurij Dalmatin's translation of the Bible (top).

Among the mountains in the Upper Savinja Valley, whose peaks reach above 2000 m, are also several mountain valleys (top right).

In past times, Gornji Grad (middle right) was a popular holiday resort. The town in the Dreta valley, also called the Zadrečka Valley, boasts a fresh mountain climate. It is a starting point for excursions to the Menina and other excursion spots.

Ljubno ob Savinji has a rich tradition in tourism. Every year they organize the traditional folk event called "flosarski bal".

The Logar Valley (top) is one of the most beautiful mountain valleys in those parts.

is joined by the Ljubnica brook which springs under Komen (1684 m).

The Savinja valley narrows after Ljubno. The Savinja current is already wilder. The valley slightly widens at Luče ob Savinji where the Lučnica brook flows from the tributary Podvolovjek valley. In this part, the Savinja valley cuts deep between the steep slopes of Ojstrica (2350 m) and Velika planina in the west, and of Veliki Rogatec (1557 m) in the east. Not far from Luče we can see the steep slope of Raduha (2062 m) reaching to the sky.

Under Ojstrica begins the tributary alpine valley Robanov kot from which flows the Bela brook, cascading down into the Savinja.

The Logar Valley (Logarska dolina) is so uniquely shaped that hardly any other valley in the Julian Alps can match it. The valley bottom is wide and green while the slopes are steep and rocky, surrounded by the magnificent Grintovci covered with numerous snow fields. Right at the end of the valley is the Rinka waterfall dropping for 80 m over a rocky wall. The parallel side valley Matkov kot is also very interesting.

Šoštanj

Šoštanj lies on the plain by the Paka below the ruins of the Pusti grad castle which used to control the road through the narrow Paka valley. It was first mentioned in writing in 1199, in 1384 it was granted a market charter. At that time it was the center of the Šalek Valley. Today it has the largest thermal power complex in Slovenia. Both, the Šoštanj and Velenje areas are rich in coal which is still mined today.

At Šoštanj, the Paka enters a narrow gorge. In the west slope of Skom (721 m) is the Rotovnik cave (Rotovnikova jama) known for its aragonite crystals resembling hedgehogs *(aragonitni ježki)*.

It can be visited by tourists. Only a few kilometers from Šoštanj, in the Toplica valley, lies the thermal spa Topolšica whose thermal spring was well-known as early as the 16th century.

In Zavodnje above Topolšica, on the slope of Petrov vrh (825 m) lies the old restored Kavčnik Farmhouse - a veritable museum and a tribute to local farm-styled architecture.

Bele vode with scattered farms and ruins of a castle lies west from Šoštanj at a height of 700 m to 900 m.

Velenje

Velenje is the center of the Šalek Valley. It developed at the foot of a steep hill atop which stands a mighty castle. The castle was first mentioned in writing in the 13th century. Today it houses a museum. Buildings only started to grow in 1951 due to the needs of the mine. Since then it has developed into a nice modern green town with a lot to offer. A special touch is added by the Tourist Lake (Turistično jezero) with a surface of 1 km2 and Lake Škalce (Škalsko jezero) with a surface of 16 hectares.

A road from Velenje leads through the Paka gorge past Huda luknja to the Mislinja valley. Before the road leaves the valley it passes through a short tunnel under the hill above which lie the ruins of the Šalek Castle. The valley got

The Šalek Castle was first mentioned in the 13th century. It was abandoned in the 18th century and today there are only ruins left of the former fortress (top left).

The restored and well tended Velenje Castle (top right) looks like an irregular square fortress. It houses the collections of the Velenje Museum. After its turbulent history the castle now has a peaceful cultural mission.

Although the shore of Lake Velenje is "adorned" by the thermo power complex at Šoštanj, constant underground inflow of fresh water keeps it surprisingly clean. On the shore developed a veritable recreational center. In the summer, the lake is full of bathers.

The Ljubija gorge near Bele Vode hides waterfalls, and high up in steep rocks along Hudi potok we find the Morova zijalka cave. Archaeologists found Stone Age remains in it. Near by is also the restored Kavčnik farmhouse (bottom and middle right).

its name from the castle. From the same junction there is a road leading south via Kavče and Andraž to Polzela in the Lower Savinja Valley, and another one east to Dobrna and Celje.

Vojnik

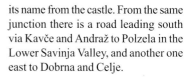

The small Hudinja River carves out the picturesque Socka gorge on its journey from southern slopes of Pohorje Massif. Low hills stretching along both banks further down the stream shut off the Celje basin in the north. From a side valley under Paški Kozjak comes the Dobrnica brook, a tributary of the Hudinja. At their confluence lies the village of Strmec and a bit further south, already in the Celje basin, Vojnik which was given a market charter in 1306. At Vojnik, a road branches off to the northeast leading via Frankolovo and Stranice to Zreče and Slovenske Konjice.

The valley between Konjiška gora and Stenica (1091 m) used to be an important passage protected by two castles - the Frankolovo Castle and Lindenški grad Castle whose ruins still stand high up on the slope of Stenica.

Dobrna

In the valley of the tiny Dobrna river, at the village of Lemberg near Strmec, is the Lemberg Castle and further up the valley lies Dobrna. The Dobrna spa was already known by the Romans. Written sources mention it only in 1428 and the tourism did not take off before 1612. Above the spa lie the ruins of the Kačnik Castle and there is another castle of a more recent origin in the Dobrna village. A kilometer and a half upstream is the Guttcnegg Castle, which is also called Dobrnica.

Among the hills stretching from the Celje basin to Dobrna lies in a shallow valley the lake Šmartinsko jezero. Its very rugged shore is 8800 metres long!

Zreče

The Dravinja River springs from numerous sources scattered under Ovčarjev vrh (1286 m) and in the ravines around the village of Skomarje. It is joined by the Ločnica brook, whose source is under Rogla, and numerous other smaller streams. The first village in the valley is Loška gora. Right after the village the valley widens and there sits Zreče which has been using the river's water power for centuries. In the surroundings old Bronze Age settlements were discovered. Zreče has developed incredibly after the WW II. Today it is a nice modern town, attractive for tourists.

Zrečans have built a on modern sports and tourist resort Rogla (1517). On Adamov vrh (1260 m) is a tower with excellent views. The whole southern slope of Pohorje is scattered with isolated farms and small villages up to a height of 1100 meters.

The Žiče monastery (top pictures) is the oldest Carthusian monastery in non-Romance Europe. It was built in the second half of the 12th century and its decline began at the end of the 18th century. Its ruins are being slowly reconstructed.

Slovenske Konjice (middle right) is an attractive tourist spot. It is a starting point for excursions to Konjiška gora and Brinjeva gora, and there are also quite some castles and wine cellars in the area which are bound to improve your mood.

Slovenske Konjice, the home of excellent white wine Konjičan, is also a famous wine district (bottom right).

Slovenske Konjice

The town lies in the Dravinja valley under the steep slope of Konjiška gora (924 m). On its slope, above Pristava, are the ruins of Old Castle (Stari grad). The town was granted a market charter in the 13th century and today it is the center of the upper part of the Dravinja valley. It has developed around the junction of the old road linking Ljubljana and Maribor, and the side road leading down the Dravinja valley. The new motorway bypassed it.

Between Žička gora (420 m) and the Homec hill sits the village of Žiče. From the side valley behind Konjiška gora flows the Žičnica brook. In its valley lie the ruins of the 12th century Žiče monastery. The monastery surrounded by mighty walls, is now under reconstruction.

Podravje (The Drava region)

Maribor

Maribor is the second-largest Slovene city situated at the mouth of the Drava Valley between the Kozjak range and the Pohorje Massif. To the south of the city stretches the Drava Plain (Dravsko polje) and to the northeast the wine-growing Slovenske Gorice. In Maribor the Drava is crossed by an important road linking Vienna to Trieste and another one leading from Koroška to Croatia. The water power of the Drava river and position at the crossroads of important routes brought Maribor a fast economic growth.

In the 12th century they built a castle atop Piramida to control the roads, and around the river-crossing developed a settlement which was soon fortified with walls and defense towers. During the Turkish invasions its development almost stopped.

In 1846 Maribor was the first Slovene town to be reached by the railway and 20 years later it became an important railway crossing, which brought it great prosperity.

Due to the ally bombardments, the city was partly destroyed during the WW II, but it flourished afterwards and it still does today. It grew along the main roads leading into the city and on the right bank of the Drava right to the foot of the Pohorje Massif. Today it has over 200.000 inhabitants.

The gymnasium was established in 1758 and today it is a university city. The Maribor Museum is one of the richest in Slovenia. The Acqarium in the city park is also worth visiting.

Right before the beginning of the lower part of the Drava valley, at Kamnica, there is a hydro power station with the Mariborsko jezero dam. Further down the Drava lies Mariborski otok, a popular recreational resort with open swimming pools.

From one of the suburbs, Radvanje, there is a cable car leading to the top of Mariborsko Pohorje where we find a

There are quite some narrow streets and passages leading from the center of Maribor to Lent (top left).

Maribor has a well preserved and almost completely restored old town core. You can still see the remains of ancient town walls and the city is adorned with a number of green oases and a huge city park. In the middle of Glavni trg is the plague pillar (top right) and among the buildings around Glavni trg the Town Hall (Rotovž) sticks out.

The vine growing on Lent is called Stara trta and has been there for over 400 years (middle right). It has become a wine symbol of Maribor and the wine-growing Slovenia. And an older vine can't be found anywhere else in the world.

In Pristan, another part of Lent, there are numerous cultural and entertaining events taking place in summer.
In the center of Maribor is also a huge, over 200 years old wine cellar. Wine is very much at home here and Styrians are merry people. Hills stretching from the city to the Austrian border are covered with vineyards and the wine cellars offer so many delicacies that you might find it hard to say good-bye to the area.

winter sports center with large skiing grounds.

By the main road from Ljubljana, near Betnava lies the Betnava Castle (Betnavski grad) which is already on the Drava plain. To the north of the city lead a road and a railroad via Košaki and Pesnica to Šentilj, the nearby border crossing with Austria. At Pesnica, a road branches off and leads through the valley of the Pesnica river to Lenart in the Slovenske Gorice and further on to Pomurje (the Mura Region). From another suburb, Tezno, a road leads along the Drava to Ptuj and further on to Zagreb in Croatia.

Ruše

In the lower Drava Valley, the Drava is dammed by the Fala hydro power station dam. The hydro power station at Fala was the first on the Drava river, built in 1918. From the dam to Maribor the valley bottom is gravely sandwiched between steep wooded slopes of the Pohorje and of the Kozjak. At the foot of the Pohorje lies Ruše which was settled already by the Illyrians. Ruše had a gymnasium as early as 1645 which remained open until 1758. Despite that Ruše has never been a market town.

The Drava Plain

The Drava Plain (Dravsko polje) is a vast triangular gravel pit deposited over the millennia by the Drava. Numerous streams flowing from the Pohorje have also had their share in shaping it. At the foot of the Pohorje, between Hoče and Polskava lie several villages. The Maribor Airport, today mostly used for cargo transports, is also on the Drava Plain.

Slovenska Bistrica

The town, already inhabited by the Romans, developed by the main road linking Maribor and Ljubljana. It acquired the status of a market town in the 11th century and the status of a town in 1313. During the Turkish invasions the town was fortified with strong walls. In the center of the town is the mighty Attems Castle (Attemsov grad).

The slopes of the Pohorje above the town represent one of the famous wine-growing districts in Slovenia. In the direction of Maribor, Ritoznoj is the best-known of numerous vineyards and wine-cellars.

Near the village of Ložnica, on one of the slopes of the Pohorje, lies Tinjska gora, famous for its remains of the Celtic burial grounds.

In Pragersko the railroad splits, one fork leads to Čakoves in Croatia and to Hungary.

There are so many hills in the Haloze (top right) that it is quite easy to get lost in them. It is also a famous wine-growing region. The center of the Haloze is Cirkulane, which lies in its eastern part.

The Štatenberg castle, which is actually more of a mansion, was built in the beginning of the 18th century for count Dizem Attems by Camesini. The square central courtyard is encompassed by four wings of the Baroque manor. Castle rooms boast impressive frescoes and the stucco work has no match in Slovenia. The manor is surrounded by a large lavish park with a fishpond.

A tradicional farm house with straw roof from the Drava Plain (bottom).

Dravinjske gorice

The Dravinja runs through the Dravinjske gorice between the wine-growing hills on one and Zbelovska gora (548 m) and Boč (979 m) on the other side. The views on a clear day are excellent from the top of Boč. Poljčane is the local center.

Right after Poljčane, at the foot of Boč, lies Studenice where they built a monastery for aristocratic women in the 13th century. During the Middle Ages the monastery was one of the richest in Štajerska. The monastery was dissolved

by the Emperor Joseph II in 1782. In the middle of the 19th century a castle was built on the same spot. Today Studenice is only a small village.

In the nearby village of Makole sits the Baroque Štatenberg Castle, built in the first half of the 18th century. In the surroundings are also the ruins of the old Štatenberg Castle whose master in the 16th century was the notorious Hungarian aristocrat, Ferenc Tahi.

The Haloze Hills

When it leaves the Dravinjske gorice, the Dravinja flows through a valley at the foot of the Haloze Hills. The Drava Plain and the valley of Dravinja are separated only by the low ridge of Ptujska gora which stretches from Štatenberg to the confluence of the Dravinja and Drava Rivers. In the valley lie Lešje and Majšperk. From those settlements lead roads via the famous Ptujska Gora to Ptuj and via the Haloze to Rogatec.

Ptujska gora was given a market charter in 1490. The 15th century church is one of the most genuine Ghotic churches in Slovenia. The Haloze are wine-growing hills stretching between the Drava and Dravinja Rivers on one and the Croatian border on the other side. Numerous streams flowing from the Haloze into the Dravinja and the Drava have cut deep valleys. In the west, the hills are higher than in the east but nevertheless they hardly ever rise above 500 meters. There is a road leading from Ptuj which crosses the Drava at the Borl Castle. The river crossing was protected already by a roman military camp.

The Borl Castle has a turbulent history. It is first mentioned in writing in 1255. Documents from 1291 describe terrible fights the castle had survived. In 1481 Hungarian king Matija Korvin had it destroyed, but it was evaluated as severely damaged in 1542 and later rebuilt. In 1706 the castle was burnt down and consequently a new one was built on the same spot. During the WW II it was, just as Rajhenburg Castle, used as a detention camp.

Ptuj

The old part of the town is squeezed between the Drava and Grajski hrib. The Ptuj Castle (Ptujski grad) is one of the largest and mightiest in Slovenia. There was a small castle on the same spot already during the Roman times. They begin to build the castle in the first millennium AD and new parts were gradually added up to the 17th century. Today the castle houses rich collections of the Ptuj Museum.

Ptuj is a monument town. The Romans called it Poetovio and many things remained from that period.

Situated at an important crossroads, Ptuj was progressing for 2000 years. But the progress stopped in the 18th century when the new road linking Ljubljana and Maribor bypassed it. After that Ptuj was only a local market for farm products and not even the railroad linking Pragersko to Čakovec in Croatia built in 1860 couldn't change that. It was only after the WW II that the town began to flourish again.

At Markovci the Drava is dammed and the dam with a surface of around 3 km2 it is the largest dam in Slovenia.

All the way from Ptuj, between Slovenske gorice and the Drava, stretches the Ptuj Plain (Ptujsko Polje). In the east-west direction it is crossed by the canal of the hydro power station Formin. From the Pesnica valley in Slovenske gorice flows the Pesnica which turns on the Ptuj Plain and flows into the Drava at Ormož. In the middle of the plain, at the mouth of the Pesnica valley, is Dornava. The village is known for its Baroque mansion house, built in 1743 and surrounded by a large park.

Ptuj, the museum town, is like an island rising from the Drava river (top right). The Ptuj castle housing the collections of the Ptuj Museum dominates over the old town core.

Every year at Mardi Gras, Ptuj organizes a massive carnival, undoubtedly the largest in Slovenia. Typical of the Ptuj region and also of the carnival is kurent (small pictures above), a creature from the other world. It is supposed to be a sign of spring, fertility and new life. But kurent is wrapped in mystery, nobody knows which ancient times and beliefs it came from and what are its true intentions.

Velika Nedelja (right) was a commendam of the German knights. There is a romantic legend associated with the origins of the Velika Nedelja Castle: Crusaders helped Frederick of Ptuj in its military march against the enemy army of the Magyar king Emerik. Frederick's army won on Easter Sunday (also called Velika Nedelja - the "big Sunday" in Slovene). Frederick stuck the crusaders' flag in the soil and named the place Velika Nedelja after the occasion. The land was only presented to the crusaders by his son, Frederick II.

Ormož

Ormož sits on the fringe of the Slovenske gorice, right above the Drava on which runs the state border with Croatia. It was settled already in the first century BC, At first by the Ilyirians and later by the Romans. At the end of the 12th century a defence tower, the base for the Ormož Castle, was built. Ormož acquired the status of a town in 1331. During the Turkish invasions the castle was the most important fortification in Styria.

Near Ormož is the village of Velika Nedelja with a big church atop the hill above the village. Next to it is a 17th century castle. In 1119 those parts came into the possession of Teutonic Knights who later on acquired huge estates and ruled over the area for centuries.

The eastern part of Slovenske gorice above Ormož is a famous wine-growing district. From Ormož, through the Pavlovski potok valley, lead a road and a railroad to Ljutomer. Gentle hills are covered with vineyards. Clustered settlements are scarce but the road is lined with farmhouses. The best-known town is Jeruzalem, renowned for its premium white wines. A visitor can follow a well marked wine route through the region.

Lenart v Slovenskih goricah

Lenart was built on a low terrace above the Pesnica valley. It only developed in the 15th century. In the

Through Jeruzalem (top right) and the wine-growing hills of Slovenske gorice leads a wine road. White wine coming from vineyards between Ljutomer and Ormož is definitely the best in Slovenia. It is the home of noble wines known and appreciated all over the world.

Sveta Trojica is a settlement in the heart of the Slovenske gorice. It sits on a low ridge above Gradiško jezero (small picture, top right). If you are in the search of carp, pike, pike-perch or sheatfish trophy try the Radehova and Pristava fishponds near Lenart.

Lenart is the only important center in the Slovenske gorice. It was built on a rounded ridge above the Pesnica river. Lenart is famous for horse racing and competitions which are organized several times a year (middle right).

The Slovenske gorice is full of sunflowers which are used for extracting oil (bottom right).

church, dating from the same century, is the tomb of the Herberstein family who owned the Hrastovec Castle, which is famous for its numerous witch trials, most of which took place in the 17th century. Lenart was under the rule of the Hrastovec Castle as well. Today the castle houses a sanatorium for mentally retarded patients. Sadly, there are several other castles in Slovenia experiencing the same fate as Hrastovec.

The castle is situated in the Pesnica valley and can easily be spotted from the road linking Maribor and Lenart. There are some larger lakes in the valley which are actually all dams on Pesnica. Since the Pesnica used to flood the valley frequently, several dams were built and the floods stopped.

Not far from Lenart, on the edge of the Pesnica valley, by the road leading from Lenart to Ormož, is the lake Gradiško jezero. On the terrace above it lies another important Slovenske gorice market town: Gradišče. On top of the hill in the village sits the 17th century Baroque Church of the Holy Trinity, with three belfries. The settlement is also called Sveta Trojica (the Holy Trinity), after the church. It did not receive its market charter until 1872.

Pomurje
(The Mura Region)

Extraordinary hospitality of the locals and mysterious flat landscape are simply enchanting. Excellent traditional dishes and numerous thermal springs attract tourists. It is a land of lazy rivers, mysterious moors, fishponds, and rich in game. It is a place where hunters and fishermen can still find species that have become rare elsewhere in Europe.

Murska Sobota

The center of The Mura Region is Murska Sobota, sitting away from the Mura river in the middle of the Ravensko Plain, the largest plain in Slovenia. A medieval settlement was there already in the 11th century. Murska Sobota was given a town charter in 1479 by the Hungarian king Matija Korvin. Murska Sobota gained some importance only in the first half of the 20th century and became an important regional center after the WW II.

From the west hills over the Ravensko Plain flows the small Lendava River, joined on the plain by numerous streams flowing from Goričko. Beltinci, Turnišče, Dobrovnik and other smaller villages with typical small Panonian-styled houses line the roads. Despite the vast plain and fertile soil farms are usually small and their fields scattered.

Gornja Radgona

The Mura river enters Slovenia at Ceršak, only a few kilometers from the Šentilj border crossing. The state border with Austria runs on the Mura almost as far as Radenci.

Gornja Radgona sits on the southern bank of the Mura. It received a town charter in 1265. Although in the middle Ages it was built as a unified settlement it got split in two by the border on the Mura after the WW I. The Slovene part of the town is a former suburb with a medieval castle.

The area whose center is Murska Sobota (top) used to be called Okroglina (a circle). In the middle of the large town park is the Sobota Manor with a beautiful Baroque portal (bottom right). Portal adorned with two Atlases was made by a master who followed Magyar patterns and is among the most beautiful in Slovenia. The restored Manor houses a museum collection.

Lake Negova (top right), with a surface of 5 hectares, is hidden among the murmuring forests of the Slovenske gorice. The lake and the nearby village of Negova are becoming more and more popular among tourists.

Origins of Gornja Radgona are closely connected with the 12th century castle (middle right) on Grajski grič. Since the town is surrounded by orchards and vineyards, it has traded in wine since ever.
On Šlebingerjev breg grows the largest vine in Slovenia, over 100 cm in circumference.

The Apače Plain stretches among the Mura, the Slovenske Gorice and Gornja Radgona. On a rock in the westernmost part of the plain is the mighty Cmurek Castle which used to control the crossing over the river. There is a bridge here today and the Trate border crossing near Austrian Mureck (Cmurek). The castle is one of the oldest and most famous, but unfortunately it shares the fate of Hrastovec and a number of other castles in Slovenia.

From the road linking Gornja Radgona and Lenart a side road branches off at Ihova and leads through the Ščavnica valley to Negova. There you'll find an 11th century castle which is sadly falling apart.

Thermal springs in Radenci were discovered in 1833, but the tourism did not develop until 1871 when they began to use them for medical purposes. The thermal water is considered one of the best in Europe and today, springs are surrounded by a modern holiday village.

Although the hills of Goričko are low, they are not suitable for growing vine. Maybe that is the main reason behind strongly developed fruit growing. Diligent hands of the locals work the fertile land (right).

Ljutomer

Ljutomer developed on the edge of the Mura Plain, at the foot of Slovenske Gorice. Around the original defence tower a castle was built first and then the settlement. It received its market rights in 1625 but it did not acquire the status of a town until 1927.

On the Mura Plain, by the Mura, sits Veržej which received its market rights in the 14th century. Serbian Uskoks, who escaped from the Turks, had a castle in Veržej. Floating mills on this part of the Mura give the river a unique charm, as well as the thermal spas on the plain which lead tourist development of the area.

Lendava

Lendava sits at the foot of the Lendavske gorice and Dolgovaške gorice. The Romans have built there a military camp and called it Halicanum. For long centuries this part of Slovenia has been under Hungarian thumb.

A border crossing with Hungary is at Dolga vas near Lendava and only a few kilometers south is Mursko središče in Croatia. On this narrow strip of land we find some typical Panonian villages. The easternmost Slovenian village is Pince.

The Ledava River follows almost a straight line over the Dubrovniško dolinsko and Lendavsko dolinsko plains and crosses the state border in the easternmost part of Slovenia, at the triple border of Slovenia, Hungary and Croatia. A narrow strip of land between the Mura and the Ledava, uninhabited and mostly marshy, cuts among the two neighbouring countries.

Lake Ledava is slowly sinking into the dark of the night, but its shores are noisy as if you were in the fiercest battle. During the hunting season for low game it is not exactly safe to walk through thick reeds along the shore since the lake attracts fishermen and hunters from everywhere.

The Mura used to be full of floating mills. One of the few that still stands and works is near Veržej (middle right). Water wheel is placed on two floating pontoons and connected with a belt to the real mill on the shore.

The castle (bottom right) was for centuries the administrative center of Goričko. Its irregular ground plan is perfectly matched with the configuration of the ground. Today it is overgrown with lush greenery of the castle park.

Goričko

Almost half of Prekmurje (the Transmuraland) is Goričko, low, gently sloping hills with equally high oblong and rounded ridges. Sometimes round peaks rise above them, and in some other parts they change into wide passes. The area borders Austria and Hungary. One third of Goričko is

covered by mostly pine forests, but there are also a lot of beech, oak and alder trees to be found. This is an orchard land, since the soil is not suitable for vine.

The Ledava river flowing from Austria flows into a big dam, Ledavsko jezero.

On the ridge between the Grački potok and Radovski potok brooks sits the village of Grad (castle) which got its name from a mighty medieval castle. The castle is first mentioned in writing in 1214. Today it is neglected and parts of it are destroyed. In the castle chapel is a museum room with rare remains of a once rich inventory.

Chapter Index

Index

63

Bibliography

Atlas Slovenije, 1992. Mladinska knjiga in Geodetski zavod Slovenije, Ljubljana.
Telefonski imenik Slovenije 1996/97, Telekom Slovenije, Ljubljana.
Gorenjska - vodnika, 1997, Chvatal Matjaž, Založba Turistika, Kranj.
Slovenija - turistični vodnik, 1995, Chvatal Matjaž, samozaložba, Ljubljana.
Lovne vode Slovenije, 1994, Štefe Brane, Chvatal Matjaž, samozaložba, Ljubljana.
Slovenija in njeni kraji, 1964, Planina France, Prešernova družba, Ljubljana.
Počitnice v Sloveniji, 1987, Šober Milenko, Potočnik Cveta, etc., Centralni zavod za napredek gospodinjstva, Ljubljana.
Slapovi v Sloveniji, 1983, Ramovš Anton, Slovenska matica, Ljubljana.
Domače obrti na Slovenskem, 1989, Bogataj Janez, Državna založba Slovenije, Ljubljana.
Sto naravnih znamenitosti Slovenije, 1988, Skoberne Peter, Prešernova družba, Ljubljana.
Sto slovenskih krajev, 1994, Kladnik Darinka, Prešernova družba, Ljubljana.
Zakladi Slovenije, 1979, Kmecl Matjaž, Cankarjeva založba, Ljubljana.
Gradovi na Slovenskem, 1989, Stopar Ivan, Cankarjeva založba, Ljubljana.
Prospektni material Turističnih društev in drugih ponudnikov turističnih storitev v Sloveniji.

The booklets has been translated into
Slovenian, English, German and Italian.

Questions about Slovenia

It provides answers to numerous questions about Slovenia and
Slovenes living in their native and neighbouring countries as well
as abroad.

The booklet is about holidays, wine, the sea, mountains, forests,
rivers, early and recent history, cuisine, tourism, the legal system,
politics, humour, envy, cleverness, sadness, drinking problems,
superstition...

*(112 pages, 150 colour photographs, a map, format 11.5 x 22.5
cm, paperback)*

Slovenian Cooking

The booklet details 140 old and not so old national dishes,
which cherish a rich tradition in Slovenia. Throughout the
centuries some of them have managed to preserve themselves to
this day. A different ground structure and varying climate in some
areas as well as economic and cultural factors have contributed
their part in creating 40 culinary regions. These are characterized
by different eating habits and typical dishes.

140 recipes of both very well and less known Slovene dishes
have been collected by a chef, Andrej A. Fritz, 2001

(64 pages, format 11.5 x 22.5 cm, paperback)

Slovenia - Guide

The booklet is a brief presentation of Slovenia and its principal
characteristics. The texts are complemented by 150 colour
photographs and a small but clear map of Slovenia.

The introductory part is general, and includes basic information
about Slovenia, its tourism, history, arts and crafts, cuisine… The
following chapters present individual regions, bigger towns and
other sights of interest.

*(112 pages, 150 colour photographs, a map, format 11.5 x
22.5 cm, paperback)*

A road map of Slovenia and Istria

Maps of the following city centres: Ljubljana, Maribor, Celje,
Kranj and Koper

(scale:1:300,000, format 100 x 70)

Trstenik 101 SI-4204 Golnik
e-mail: info@zalozba-turistika.si
www.zalozba-turistika.si

MESTNA OBČINA
KRANJ

The grey rock the ancient town of Kranj is perched on offered settlement to people as early as few centuries BC. The Slovenes settled it in the 6th and 7th centuries and built there a strong community to which testifies the largest burial ground from that period in Slovenia, which was unearthed at Glavni trg. After losing its sovereignty, Kranj became the seat of the Kranj County with its own border count, giving name to the whole area (Kranj ska) which was a political and administrative unit until the downfall of the Habsburg Empire (1918). In the Middle Ages, it became an important trade centre which brought it a town charter already in the 13th century. Development of iron foundries in Carniola and Carinthia in the 16th century influenced its economic growth, since trade and transport increased substantially. First manufactures appeared in the first half of the 19th century, and industry emerged at the end of the 19th century. Kranj thus became the economic, trade, cultural, administrative, educational and ecclesiastic centre of the Gorenj ska region.

Kranj is a university town with the Faculty of Organisational Sciences. There are eight secondary and nine primary schools in the commune. Kranj is also called `Prešeren's Town' since the greatest Slovene poet, dr. France Prešeren (1800 - 1849), lived, worked and found his peace here. Several buildings and institutions were named after him such as Prešernova hiša in the centre which has been turned into the museum, and the main Kranj theatre, Prešernovo gledališče, for example. The town čemetery also carries his name.

Kranj boasts one of the nicest Olympic swimming pools in Europe. Good sports conditions and facilities have enabled many a sportsman to achieve excellent results on a national or world scale.

Kranj's economy with a constantly growing quality of its products is a successful competitor on the world market. Well developed are mostly electronic, rubber, shoemaking and textile industries. Middle-sized and small businesses and crafts are also gaining importance. People in Kranj are diligent and persistent and consequently the town boasts companies which are successful all over the world.

A number of archaeological and other monuments, the most prominent are Plečnik arcades with a fountain, the Town Hall, the Pavšler and Mitničar houses and Kislstein Castle, make the old town core beautiful and interesting for touristš. Former town cemetery at the edge of the old town core has been turned into a wonderful park called Prešernov gaj. There you will find monuments to the Slovene poets France Prešeren and Simon Jenko, and the oldest anti-Fascist monument in the world, dating from 1930. The parish Church of St. Cantianus and comrades, a Ghotic monument, is one of the first Slovene town churches. The town core is also adorned by the Church of the Holy Rosary and Church of Sts. Sebastian and Rok on Pungert, while the town walls and the Škrlovec fortress offer lovely views. In Glavni trg you will find the Town Fountain, the top of which is adorned by a golden ball with an eagle, the symbol of Kranj. From the Middle Ages on, Kranj has been built in the typical pyramidal form, emphasized by the Kranj belfries, while the basic side was shaped by the town walls with defense towers. Kranj is one of the few Slovene towns that managed to preserve its original town silhouette.

Kranj suburbs and countryside, offering a number of possibilities for excursions and walks, are also interesting for tourists. In the close vicinity of the town are situated two excursion spots: Sv. Jošt and Šmarjetna gora with the Bellevue Hotel and the reconstructed Church of St. Margaret. The views from the hilltops of Kranj and its surroundings and the whole Gorenj ska Plain, are astonishing.

The Bobovek area near Kranj and the Kokra River Canyon, which constantly attract visitors with their beauties, were declared natural monuments a few years ago.

One of the most valuable protocol objects in Slovenia is the Brdo Castle with a wonderful park and sports grounds, where historical tradition and modern times meet.

Any visitor can find something for himself in the Gorenj ska capital and its surroundings, be it a business deal, a visit to one of the numerous cultural or natural sights or just a chat with economical and hospitable locals in one of the many friendly pubs in Kranj.

EVENTS:

- Slovenial Drama Week (spring)
- Summer in Kranj
- International Jumping week in Kranj (June)
- Cycling Race for the Kranj Grand Prix (June)
- International Swimming Championsip in Kranj (June)
- The Gorenjsko Competittion in Accordian Playing at Besnica (June)
- The Kranj Night (end of July-beginning of August)
- New Year's Eve Run and New Year's Eve Party in the old town core (December)

INFORMATION:
Tourist Information Centre Kranj,
Koroška cesta 29, 4000 KRANJ,
Tel./Fax: (+386) 04 236 30 30, Fax: 04 236 30 31

CASINÒ
BLED

ODPRTO VSAK DAN - GEÖFNED JEDEN TAG - APERTO OGNI GIORNO
OUVERT CHAQUE JOUR - OPEN EVERY DAY
PON - ČET 17.^{00} - 05.^{00}
PETEK, SOBOTA IN NEDELJA - FRIDAY, SATURDAY AND SUNDAY:
15.^{00} - 05.^{00}

ROULETTE - BLACK JACK - POKER - SLOT MACHINES

CASINO Bled d.d., Cesta svobode 15, 4260 Bled,
Tel.: (+386) 04 574 18 11, Fax: 04 574 43 81
http://www.casino-bled.si - info@casino-bled.si

Ribčev Laz 48, 4265 Bohinjsko jezero
Tel.: (+386) 04 572 33 70, Fax: 04 572 33 30

TURISTIČNO DRUŠTVO BOHINJ

E-mail: tdbohinj@bohinj.si, http://www.bohinj.si

1000 beds in private rooms and apartments in all
Bohinj area. The Bohinj Tourist Office is also the
main information point for all visitors to Bohinj.

www.sobec.si

camping
Šobec
LESCE Slovenija

Your Place in Nature

Camping Šobec
Šobčeva cesta 25, SI-4248 Lesce
Tel.: 00386 4 53 53 700
Fax: 00386 4 53 53 700
E-mail: sobec@siol.net

www.radovljica.si

RADOVLJICA

(491 m, administrative, educational, cultural and business center of Radovljica commune).

The Manor houses the Radovljica Festival, the oldest festival of old music in Slovenia.
www.festival-radovljica.amis.net

Traditional Events

February
Mardi Gras Carnival

April
The 4th Linhart's Theatre Marathon

1st May
Labour Day events at Šobec

June
Venus' Path: Archery Tournament of the Gašper Lamberger Knight Order

Venus' Path: "Midsummer Eve – celebrating Midsummer Eve at the Kamen castle near Begunje

June, July
"Radolško poletje": musical, theatre and puppet theatre events

July
Venus' Path: The Blacksmith Fair in Kropa

Tourist places:
Begunje, Brezje, Kropa, Lesce and Radovljica

Tourist information:
- Turistično društvo Radovljica
  Kranjska 13, Radovljica, tel.: 04 531 53 00
- Turistično društvo Lesce
  Alpska cesta 58, Lesce, tel.: 04 535 37 00

Lesce has a sport airport, a hippodrome, a beautiful golf course and the Šobec camping site

August
'Radovljica Festival - international festival of ancient music

September
Entertaining event by Forever Young Boys at Radovljica

December
Linhart's events Away, away with the Old Year

All year
Sports events

Pilgrimage Church of Our Lady at Brezje
www.brezje.si

Begunje are known for the hostage museum, the Avseniks and for reviving medieval culture for tourists, called "Venus' Path" at Kamen Castle
www.begunje.si

Kropa is the cradle of blacksmiths.kropa.si

LINHART'S TOWN OF CULTURE INVITES YOU

HOTELI PALACE

PORTOROŽ
PORTOROSE
Slovenija

The Thermae with a sea-view
Welcome in Portorož - a renown
tourist resort with a pleasant
Mediterranean climate and a
hundred years old spa tradition.

Grand Hotel Palace ****, Apollo
Hotel ****, Mirna Hotel **** and
Neptun Hotel ****

Information and reservations:
HOTELI PALACE d.d., Obala 43,
6320 Portorož
Tel.: +386/5/6969 001, 6969 002,
Fax: +386/5/6969 003
e-mail: marketing@hoteli-palace.si
http://www.hoteli-palace.si

TERME PALACE
THALASSO CENTRE
mud and algae packs and baths, brine bath, whirlpool, thalaxion, Vichy and multi-jet massage, inhalation, …
MASSAGE CENTRE
hand massage, feet reflex massage, lymph drainage, Shiatsu, Thai and Tuina massage, Aroma massage, Ayurveda massage
PHYSIOTHERAPY CENTRE
Different kinds of electrotherapy, individual therapeutic exercises, thermotherapy, magnetotherapy, …
MEDICAL BEAUTY CENTRE
face beauty care, face mask, pedicure, manicure, electrolipolysis, electrogym, pressotherapy, …
THERMAL RECREATIONAL CENTRE
swimming-pools with thermo-mineral water, saunas, tepidarium, fitness centre, solarium
acupuncture, medical examinations and services

*Listen to the sea and it will
reveal to you the secret of
health and beauty.*

Park *Škocjanske jame*

Javni zavod
Park Škocjanske jame,
Škocjan 2, SI - 6215 Divača
Informacije: Tel.: 05/7632-
840, faks 05/7632-844
E-mail: Psj@psj.gov.si
www.park-skocjanske-jame.si

**URNIK OBISKOV
ORARIO DELLE VISITE
VISITS
BESUCHE
LES VISITES**

VI., VII., VIII., IX.: 10.00,
11.30, 13.00, 14.00, 15.00,
16.00, 17.00h

IV.,V.,X. : 10.00, 13.00, 15.30h

XI., XII., I., II., III.: 10.00 in
13.00h,

- NEDELJA IN PRAZNIKI
TUDI OB 15.00h
- DOMENICHE, GIORNI
FESTIVI ANCHE ALLE
15.00h
- SUNDAYS, FESTIVE DAYS
ALSO AT 15.00h
- SOUNTAGS UND
FEIERTAGS AUCH UM
15.00h
- DIMANCHES ET JOURS
FERIES EN 15.00h

In 1986, their unique natural and cultural sights put the Škocjan caves on the UNESCO World Heritage list. In 1999, when they were inscribed into the Ramsar Convention, the caves became the only underground wetland in the world.

In the Škocjan Caves Regional Park you can admire extraordinary Karst landscape which, together with a system of caves, collapsed dolines and individual cultural monuments, represents typical Karst architecture.

CONVENTION ON WETLANDS
(Ramsar, Iran, 1971)